MW00570063

Create Amazing Web Pages
with HTML

SIMPLIFIED

IN FULL COLOR

VISUAL **3D** SERIES

by: maranGraphics' Development Group

Corporate Sales

Contact maranGraphics
Phone: (905) 890-3300
     (800) 469-6616
Fax: (905) 890-9434

Canadian Trade Sales

Contact Prentice Hall Canada
Phone: (416) 293-3621
     (800) 567-3800
Fax: (416) 299-2529

Visit our Web site at:
http://www.maran.com

Create Amazing Web Pages with HTML Simplified

Copyright© 1996 by maranGraphics Inc.
5755 Coopers Avenue
Mississauga, Ontario, Canada
L4Z 1R9

Canadian Cataloguing in Publication Data

Maran, Ruth, 1970-
    Create amazing Web pages with HTML simplified

(Visual 3-D series)
Written by Ruth Maran and Paul Whitehead.
Includes index.
ISBN 1-896283-25-X

1. Hypertext systems.   2. HTML (Document markup language).
3. World Wide Web (Information retrieval system).
I. Whitehead, Paul, 1965–   .   II. MaranGraphics Inc.
III. Title.   IV. Series.

QA76.76.H94M37 1996   005.75   C96-932137-6

Printed in the United States of America

10   9   8   7   6   5   4   3   2   1

All rights reserved. No part of this publication may be used, reproduced or transmitted, in any form or by any means, electronic, mechanical, photocopying, recording or otherwise, or stored in any retrieval system of any nature, without the prior written permission of the copyright holder, application for which shall be made to: maranGraphics Inc., 5755 Coopers Avenue, Mississauga, Ontario, Canada, L4Z 1R9.
This publication is sold with the understanding that neither maranGraphics Inc., nor its dealers or distributors, warrants the contents of the publication, either expressly or impliedly, and, without limiting the generality of the foregoing, no warranty either express or implied is made regarding this publication's quality, performance, salability, capacity, suitability or fitness with respect to any specific or general function, purpose or application. Neither maranGraphics Inc., nor its dealers or distributors shall be liable to the purchaser or any other person or entity in any shape, manner or form whatsoever regarding liability, loss or damage caused or alleged to be caused directly or indirectly by this publication.
maranGraphics has used their best efforts in preparing this book. As Web sites are constantly changing, some of the Web site addresses in this book may have moved or no longer exist. maranGraphics does not accept responsibility nor liability for losses or damages resulting from the information contained in this book. maranGraphics also does not support the views expressed in the Web sites contained in this book.

Trademark Acknowledgments

maranGraphics Inc. has attempted to include trademark information for products, services and companies referred to in this guide. Although maranGraphics Inc. has made reasonable efforts in gathering this information, it cannot guarantee its accuracy.

All other brand names and product names used in this book are trademarks, registered trademarks, or trade names of their respective holders. maranGraphics Inc. is not associated with any product or vendor mentioned in this book.

FOR PURPOSES OF ILLUSTRATING THE CONCEPTS AND TECHNIQUES DESCRIBED IN THIS BOOK, THE AUTHOR HAS CREATED VARIOUS NAMES, COMPANY NAMES, MAILING ADDRESSES, E-MAIL ADDRESSES AND PHONE NUMBERS, ALL OF WHICH ARE FICTITIOUS. ANY RESEMBLANCE OF THESE FICTITIOUS NAMES, COMPANY NAMES, MAILING ADDRESSES, E-MAIL ADDRESSES AND PHONE NUMBERS TO ANY ACTUAL PERSON, COMPANY AND/OR ORGANIZATION IS UNINTENTIONAL AND PURELY COINCIDENTAL.

The animated characters are the copyright of maranGraphics, Inc.

Create Amazing Web Pages

with HTML

— SIMPLIFIED —

IN FULL COLOR

VISUAL 3D SERIES

maranGraphics™

*Every maranGraphics book represents
the extraordinary vision and commitment of a unique family:
the Maran family of Toronto, Canada.*

Back Row (from left to right): *Sherry Maran, Rob Maran, Richard Maran, Maxine Maran, Jill Maran.*
Front Row (from left to right): *Judy Maran, Ruth Maran.*

Richard Maran is the company founder and its inspirational leader. He developed maranGraphics' proprietary communication technology called "visual grammar." This book is built on that technology—empowering readers with the easiest and quickest way to learn about computers.

Ruth Maran is the Author and Architect—a role Richard established that now bears Ruth's distinctive touch. She creates the words and visual structure that are the basis for the books.

Judy Maran is the Project Manager. She works with Ruth, Richard, and the highly talented maranGraphics illustrators, designers, and editors to transform Ruth's material into its final form.

Rob Maran is the Technical and Production Specialist. He makes sure the state-of-the-art technology used to create these books always performs as it should.

Sherry Maran manages the Reception, Order Desk, and any number of areas that require immediate attention and a helping hand.

Jill Maran is a jack-of-all-trades and dynamo who fills in anywhere she's needed anytime she's back from university.

Maxine Maran is the Business Manager and family sage. She maintains order in the business and family—and keeps everything running smoothly.

Oh, and three other family members are seated on the sofa. These graphic disk characters help make it fun and easy to learn about computers. They're part of the extended maranGraphics family.

Credits

Authors:
Ruth Maran & Paul Whitehead

Copy Editor & Indexer:
Kelleigh Wing

Project Manager:
Judy Maran

Editors:
Brad Hilderley
Karen Derrah

Proofreaders:
Susan Beytas
Richard Warren

Layout & Cover Design:
Christie Van Duin

Illustrators:
Tamara Poliquin
Chris K.C. Leung
Russell Marini
Ben Lee

Screen Shot Permissions:
Sherry Maran

Post Production:
Robert Maran

Acknowledgments

Thanks to the dedicated staff of maranGraphics, including Susan Beytas, Karen Derrah, Francisco Ferreira, Brad Hilderley, Ben Lee, Chris K.C. Leung, Alison MacAlpine, Michael W. M^{ac}Donald, Jill Maran, Judy Maran, Maxine Maran, Robert Maran, Sherry Maran, Russ Marini, Tamara Poliquin, Christie Van Duin, Richard Warren, Paul Whitehead and Kelleigh Wing.

Finally, to Richard Maran who originated the easy-to-use graphic format of this guide. Thank you for your inspiration and guidance.

Screen Shot Permissions

Screens That Appear Throughout The Book

Apple, the Apple logo and the Macintosh computer and screen copyright Apple Computer, Inc. Used with permission.

CyberDance screen shot used with permission.

Flower Stop screen shot used with permission. http://www.flowerstop.com

Microsoft Windows 95, Microsoft FrontPage, Microsoft Excel for Windows 95, Microsoft Word for Windows 95, MSN™, The Microsoft Network, and Microsoft Internet Explorer screen shots reprinted by permission from Microsoft Corporation. Microsoft and Windows are registered trademarks and MSN is a trademark of Microsoft Corporation.

Netscape screen shots used with permission. Netscape and Netscape Navigator are trademarks of Netscape Communications Corp.

USA TODAY Online screen shot used with permission. Copyright 1996 USA TODAY Online.

Chapter 1

Le Grand Louvre screen shots reprinted with permission.

Lynx screen shot used with permission. Lynx is copyrighted by the University of Kansas and is distributed under the GNU General Public License. Any questions concerning licensing or usage should be directed to Michael Grobe <grobe@ukans.edu>.

YAHOO! screen shot reprinted with permission. Text and artwork copyright © 1996 by YAHOO!, Inc. All rights reserved. YAHOO! and the YAHOO! logo are trademarks of YAHOO!, Inc.

Chapter 2

AIDS Memorial Quilt screen shot used with permission.

Cybertimes' Property Net screen shot used with permission.

Web user statistics used with permission from The Georgia Institute of Technology.

Le Grand Louvre screen shots reprinted with permission.

MovieWEB screen shot used with permission.

New Balance Cyberpark screen shot used with permission.

Chapter 3

Kenn Nesbitt's WebEdit screen shot used with permission.

Chapter 5

HomeOwners Finance Center screen shot used with permission.

Minor Leagues, Major Dreams screen shot used with permission.

Paint Shop Pro screen shot used with permission from JASC Inc.

Chapter 6

Paint Shop Pro screen shot used with permission from JASC Inc.

Chapter 7

Smithsonian Institution screen shot used with permission. Copyright # 1996 by Smithsonian Institution.

Chapter 9

Planet Earth Home Page screen shot used with permission.

Submit It! screen shot used with permission. Copyright 1995-1996 Submit It! Inc. All Rights Reserved.

WebStep TOP 100 screen shot used with permission.

WS_FTP screen shots used with permission.

Chapter 10

Cybertown screen shot used with permission. Cybertown images copyright Cybertown 1996.

Caligari Pioneer screen shot used with permission.

SURFERmag.com screen shot used with permission. All photos on the SURFERmag.com Web site are copyrighted and may not be used on other Web sites or other media without expressed written consent of SURFER Publications or the photographers themselves.

YAHOO! screen shot reprinted with permission. Text and artwork copyright © 1996 by YAHOO!, Inc. All rights reserved. YAHOO! and the YAHOO! logo are trademarks of YAHOO!, Inc.

Chapter 11

Best Western screen shot used with permission. Copyright 1995-1996, Best Western International, Inc. All rights reserved.

Campbell Soup Company screen shot used with permission. Copyright 1995 Campbell Soup Company. Campbell's is a registered trademark.

CNET: The Computer Network screen shot reprinted with permission from CNET: The Computer Network, copyright 1996. http://www.cnet.com

CNN Interactive screen shot used with permission. © 1996 Cable News Network Inc. All Rights Reserved.

Consumer Direct Electronics screen shot used with permission.

Discovery Channel Online screen shot used with permission.

ESPNET SportsZone screen shot used with permission.

golf.com screen shot used with permission.

Hotels and Travel on the Net screen shot used with permission.

Internet Mall screen shot used with permission.

JewelryNet screen shot used with permission.

Lycos screen shot used with permission. Copyright © 1996 Lycos, Inc. All Rights Reserved. The Lycos™ "Catalog of the Internet" Copyright © 1994, 1995, 1996 Carnegie Mellon University. All Rights Reserved. Used by permission.

National Zoo screen shot reprinted courtesy of Marc Bretzfelder, National Zoological Park, Smithsonian Institution.

Pathfinder screen shot used with permission. © 1996 Time Inc. New Media. All rights reserved. Reproduction in whole or in part without permission is prohibited. Pathfinder is a registered trademark of Time Inc. New Media.

PC Flowers & Gifts screen shot used with permission.

Perrier screen shot used with permission.

Smithsonian Institution screen shot used with permission. Copyright # 1996 by Smithsonian Institution.

Spiegel screen shot used with permission from ©Spiegel, Inc.

Veggies Unite! screen shot used with permission.

TABLE OF CONTENTS

TABLE OF CONTENTS

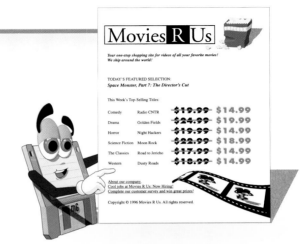

TABLE OF CONTENTS

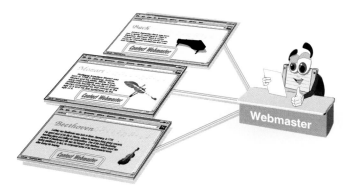

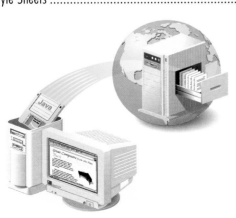

INTRODUCTION TO THE INTERNET

The Internet is often called the Net, the Information Superhighway or Cyberspace.

HISTORY

In the late 1960s, the U.S. Defense Department began the Internet as a military research project. The government created a network that covered a large geographic area and could withstand a nuclear attack. If part of the network failed, information could still find a new route around the disabled computers.

The network quickly grew to include scientists and researchers across the U.S. Eventually, schools, businesses and libraries around the world were on the Internet.

CONNECTED NETWORKS

The Internet consists of thousands of connected networks around the world. Networks allow computers to exchange information.

Each government, company and organization on the Internet is responsible for maintaining its own network.

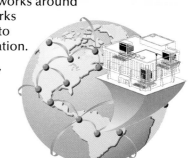

Electronic Mail

Electronic mail (e-mail) is the most popular feature on the Internet. You can exchange messages with friends, colleagues, family members, customers and even people you meet on the Internet. E-mail is fast, easy, inexpensive and saves paper.

Information

The Internet gives you access to a vast amount of information on any subject imaginable. You can review newspapers, government documents, television show transcripts, recipes, job listings, airline schedules and much more.

Thousands of companies around the world provide descriptions of their products and services on the Internet. You can buy products without ever leaving your desk.

Discussion Groups

You can join discussion groups, called newsgroups, to meet people around the world with similar interests. You can ask questions, discuss problems and read interesting stories. There are thousands of discussion groups on topics such as food, humor, music, pets, politics and sports.

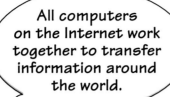

All computers on the Internet work together to transfer information around the world.

Packets

When you send information through the Internet, the information is broken down into smaller pieces, called packets. Each packet travels independently through the Internet and may take a different path to arrive at the intended destination.

When the packets arrive at the destination, the packets are reassembled.

TCP/IP

Transmission Control Protocol/Internet Protocol (TCP/IP) is a language computers on the Internet use to communicate with each other. TCP/IP divides information you send into packets and sends the packets through the Internet. When information arrives at the intended destination, TCP/IP ensures that all the packets arrived safely.

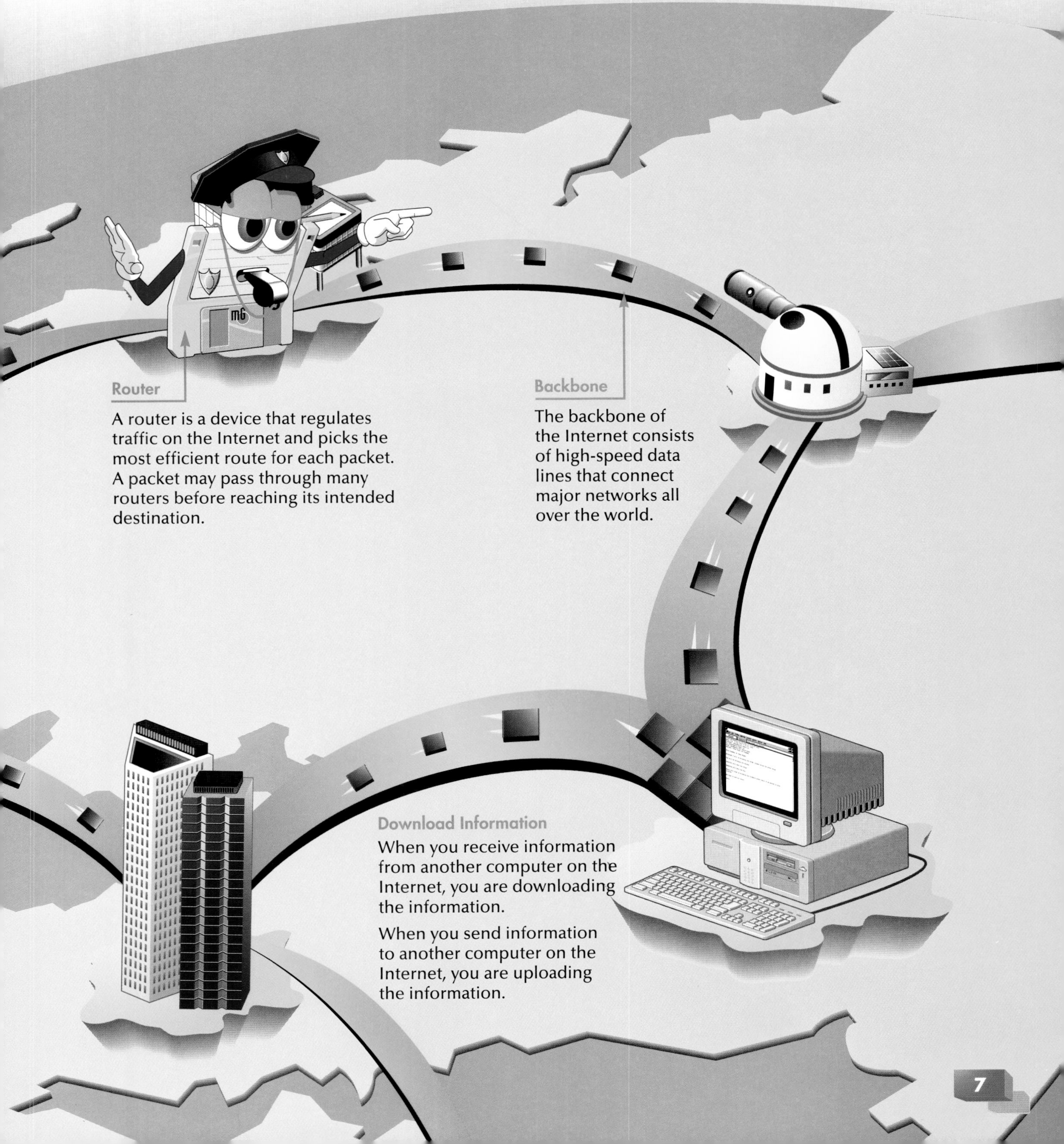

Router

A router is a device that regulates traffic on the Internet and picks the most efficient route for each packet. A packet may pass through many routers before reaching its intended destination.

Backbone

The backbone of the Internet consists of high-speed data lines that connect major networks all over the world.

Download Information

When you receive information from another computer on the Internet, you are downloading the information.

When you send information to another computer on the Internet, you are uploading the information.

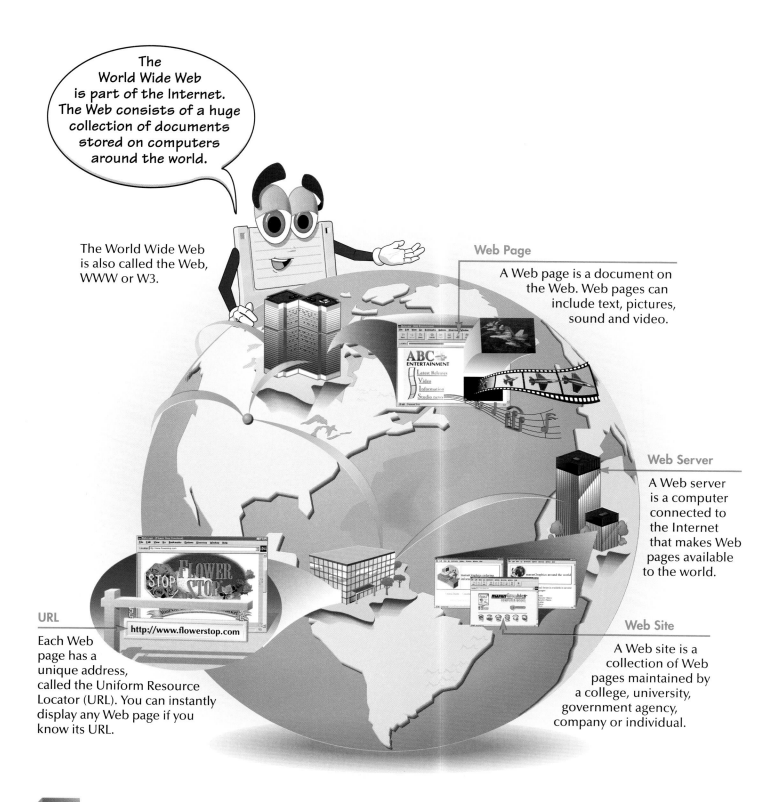

The World Wide Web is part of the Internet. The Web consists of a huge collection of documents stored on computers around the world.

The World Wide Web is also called the Web, WWW or W3.

Web Page

A Web page is a document on the Web. Web pages can include text, pictures, sound and video.

Web Server

A Web server is a computer connected to the Internet that makes Web pages available to the world.

URL

Each Web page has a unique address, called the Uniform Resource Locator (URL). You can instantly display any Web page if you know its URL.

Web Site

A Web site is a collection of Web pages maintained by a college, university, government agency, company or individual.

HYPERTEXT

Web pages are hypertext documents. A hypertext document contains highlighted text that connects to other pages on the Web. You can select highlighted text on a Web page to display a page located on the same computer or a computer across the city, country or world.

Highlighted text allows you to easily navigate through a vast amount of information by jumping from one Web page to another.

SEARCH THE WEB

Search tools were developed to help people quickly find information of interest on the Web.

Search tools let you search for a specific topic of interest or browse through categories such as arts, business or sports. Each search tool uses a different method to find and catalog Web pages. This means that each search tool may give you a slightly different result.

Some popular search tools include:

AltaVista
http://www.altavista.digital.com

Infoseek
http://www.infoseek.com

Yahoo
http://www.yahoo.com

A Web browser is a program that lets you view and explore information on the Web.

POPULAR WEB BROWSERS

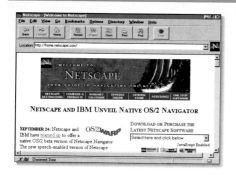

Netscape Navigator

Netscape Navigator is currently the most popular graphical Web browser. You can get Netscape Navigator at the following Web site:

http://www.netscape.com

Microsoft Internet Explorer

Microsoft Internet Explorer is currently the second most popular graphical Web browser. You can get Microsoft Internet Explorer at the following Web site:

http://www.microsoft.com

Lynx

Lynx is the most widely used text-based Web browser. This browser is fast and efficient and is commonly found on Unix systems at colleges and universities. You can get Lynx at the following Web site:

http://www.cc.ukans.edu/about_lynx/about_lynx.html

WEB BROWSER FEATURES

Bookmarks

Just as you can use bookmarks to mark your favorite pages in a book, you can use the bookmarks feature to mark your favorite pages on the Web.

The bookmarks feature lets you store the addresses of Web pages you frequently visit so you do not have to remember and constantly retype the addresses. The bookmarks feature is also called a hotlist or favorites feature.

Move Back and Forth

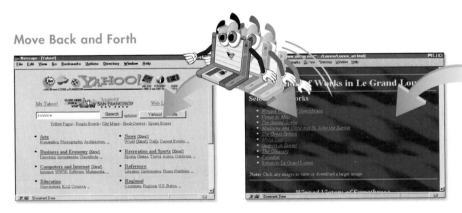

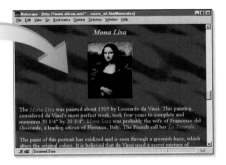

A Web browser will keep track of all the pages you have viewed since you last started the browser.

This lets you explore information without worrying about how to return to previously viewed pages.

Turn Off Images

When using a graphical Web browser, you may decide to turn off the display of images. This can save you time since images can take a while to appear on the screen.

Images On

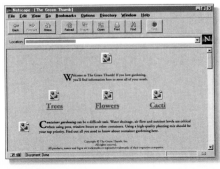

Images Off

TYPES OF CONNECTIONS

> You need to have a connection to the Internet before you can enjoy the vast amount of information available.

Modem

Most people use a modem to connect to the Internet. A modem allows computers to exchange information through telephone lines. For browsing the Web, a modem with a speed of 28,800 bps is recommended. With slower modem speeds of 14,400 bps or 9,600 bps, you will wait longer for information to appear on your screen.

ISDN

Integrated Services Digital Network (ISDN) is a high-speed digital phone line offered by telephone companies in most urban areas. ISDN lines are often used to provide companies and individuals with a high-speed connection to the Internet. ISDN transfers information up to four times faster than a modem, but is more expensive.

HOW TO CONNECT

Internet Service Provider

An Internet Service Provider (ISP) is a company that offers access to the Internet.

Many providers offer access to the Internet for a certain number of hours for a monthly fee. Other providers offer unlimited access for a flat fee.

Commercial Online Service

A commercial online service is a company that offers access to the Internet.

Most online services offer access to the Internet for a certain number of hours for a monthly fee.

Online services also offer information such as daily news, weather reports and encyclopedias. This information is well organized and easy to find, unlike information on the Internet.

Popular online services include America Online, CompuServe and The Microsoft Network.

University or Company

Universities and colleges often give students and teachers free access to the Internet. Companies often give employees free access.

CHAPTER 2

WEB PUBLISHING STRATEGY

PERSONAL

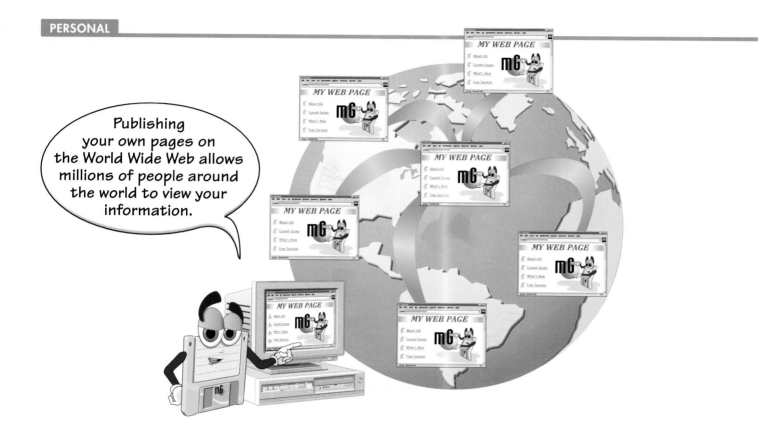

Publishing your own pages on the World Wide Web allows millions of people around the world to view your information.

Display Your Résumé

Some people use the Web to present their résumés to potential employers. By using the Web to display a résumé, you can include as much detail about yourself as you want. You can also include a picture of yourself.

Present Information of Interest

Many people use the Web to display information about a topic or range of related topics that interest them. Many Web pages are devoted to movie stars, sports teams and celebrities. People often include sounds and pictures from their favorite television shows in their Web pages.

Display Your Favorite Pictures

You can use a scanner to copy your favorite pictures or photographs onto your Web pages. A scanner is a device that reads images and text into a computer.

Learn a New Skill

In just a few years, the World Wide Web has quickly grown from a small number of Web pages to millions of pages. By learning how to create and publish pages on the Web, you gain a skill that could be valuable in your current or future career.

Have Fun

Web pages do not need to have a specific purpose. You can create your own Web pages just for fun. Many people create Web pages about their families, vacations or pets.

REASONS FOR PUBLISHING WEB PAGES

A company can place pages on the World Wide Web to inform the public about the company and the products and services it offers.

Some companies spend millions of dollars to create very large Web sites that are visited by thousands of people every day. People often pay to place advertisements on these popular commercial sites.

Shopping

Web pages allow companies to display descriptions and pictures of the products and services they offer. Many companies also allow you to use their Web pages to place orders for their products and services.

Announcements

Companies use Web pages to keep the public informed about new products and interesting news. Most companies display their press releases on the Web.

Technical Support

Companies often let you contact their technical support department through their Web site. If you have a problem with a product, you can send a message to the department. The department will then review your problem and send you a response by e-mail.

Job Listings

Many companies use their Web pages to advertise jobs that are available within the company. Some companies let you submit your résumé through their Web pages. Most companies also display the company history and the addresses and phone numbers of their offices.

Customer Feedback

Companies often let you fill out online questionnaires about their products and services. This lets you submit your opinions to help companies improve their products and services. Some companies also enter you into a draw for prizes when you fill out their questionnaire.

SPECIFIC SUBJECT

You can create and publish Web pages that are devoted to a specific subject or theme.

Promote an Organization

You can use your Web pages to display information about an organization or club that you belong to. You can include detailed information about the goals of the organization and a schedule of upcoming events. Some services that make pages available on the Web let nonprofit organizations display their pages free of charge.

Share Information About a Hobby

You can use your Web pages to share information about your favorite hobby or pastime with people all over the world. Many readers visit the Web pages of people with similar interests.

Share Your Knowledge

Many scientists and business professionals make their work available on the Web. If you are experienced in an area that many people are unfamiliar with, or if you have information that can help others, you can put the information on the Web.

Create a Fan Club

You can create your own celebrity fan club on the Web. If you are an admirer of a movie star or professional athlete, you can devote your Web pages to displaying information and pictures about them.

Entertain Your Readers

Many people create Web pages to entertain their readers. You can use your Web pages to display collections of jokes or humorous stories. You can also provide information, scripts, pictures and video clips from your favorite TV show or movie.

KNOW YOUR AUDIENCE

When designing Web pages, you must consider who will read the pages.

SPECIFIC AUDIENCE

You can design your Web pages to appeal to a specific audience. This will reduce the number of people who will visit your Web pages, but the people who do visit will be more likely to return on a regular basis. When designing Web pages for a specific audience, make sure you stick to the overall theme of your pages to maintain the interest of your readers.

GENERAL AUDIENCE

You can design your Web pages to appeal to a general audience. This will attract many visitors, but most of these people will only visit your pages once. When designing Web pages for a general audience, examine the available statistics about the people who use the Web.

WEB USER STATISTICS

These statistics were compiled by The Georgia Institute of Technology in April 1996. The latest statistics can be found at the following Web site:

http://www.cc.gatech.edu/gvu/user_surveys

Age

The average age of people who use the Web is 33 years.

Gender

Over 68% of people who use the Web are male.

Income

The average income of people who use the Web is $59,000 U.S.

Language

English is the native language of over 88% of people who use the Web.

Education

Almost 57% of people who use the Web have completed college or university.

Purpose

The most popular reasons for using the Web are browsing, entertainment and work.

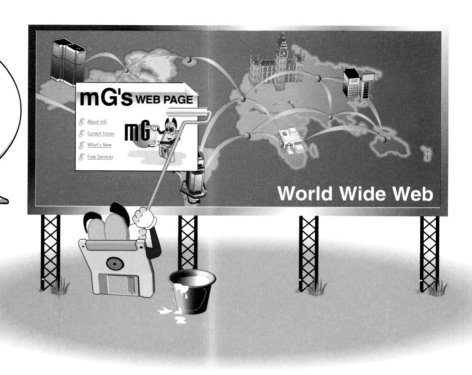

Plan Your Web Pages

Decide on a theme for your Web pages. If possible, try to make your theme unique. When planning your Web pages, first determine the goals you want the pages to accomplish and then plan the design of the pages.

Create the Text

Decide what information you want to present in your Web pages and then create the text. After you create the text, you can convert the text to HyperText Markup Language (HTML). HTML is the language used to display information on the Web.

Insert Links

A link allows readers to select an image or highlighted text to display another page on the Web. Links are one of the most important features of your Web pages since they let readers easily move through information of interest.

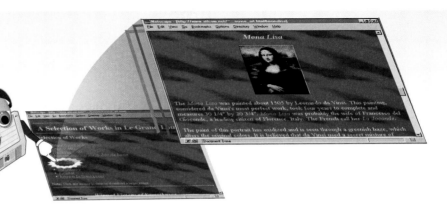

Insert Images

You can use images, such as pictures, logos or icons, to enhance the appearance of your Web pages. You can create these images on your computer, copy them from the Web or use a scanner to copy them from printed material.

Place Pages on the Web

When you finish creating your Web pages, you can transfer the pages to a service that makes pages available on the Web. Test your pages to ensure the information appears properly and all the links work. Then announce your Web pages to the world.

You should carefully plan your Web pages. Well-designed Web pages containing useful information will always be popular.

Keep a record of your original plans and ideas and refer back to them as you create your Web pages.

Decide on a Theme

Before you begin, decide what you want to accomplish with your Web pages. Determine what the main topic or theme of your Web pages will be.

Gather the Content

Collect the information you want to display in your Web pages. This information could already exist or you may have to create it yourself. While gathering the content, make sure you stick to the theme you chose for the Web pages.

Gather Supporting Information

Collect information you want to use to support your Web pages. This information may include glossaries, diagrams or the addresses of other related Web pages that will help explain your information.

Organize the Content

To organize the information you have gathered, divide the information into sections. Each section will be a separate Web page.

Each Web page should contain a different concept or idea and should have enough content to fill a single screen. Decide what supporting documents you will need for each page.

Estimate Time Involved

After you have collected and organized your information, estimate how long it will take to assemble each Web page.

Creating and maintaining a collection of Web pages can be very time-consuming, so you may want to reconsider the number and size of the Web pages before you start.

There are many things you should consider when creating and maintaining Web pages. Following a few basic guidelines will help improve your Web pages.

Examine Other Web Pages

Before you start designing your Web pages, take a close look at some of your favorite Web pages. Determine what you like about the Web pages and consider how you can use these ideas in your pages.

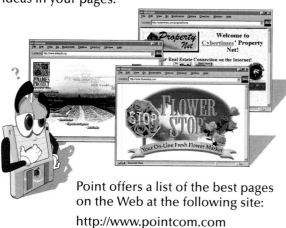

Point offers a list of the best pages on the Web at the following site:

http://www.pointcom.com

Check for Duplicates

Before you start putting your Web pages together, check to see if someone has already published Web pages containing the same information. Try to make your pages unique.

Provide a FAQ

A FAQ is a list of Frequently Asked Questions. If you plan to create Web pages dealing with technical or scientific topics, you should consider writing a FAQ. A FAQ helps quickly educate readers so they can make better use of your Web pages.

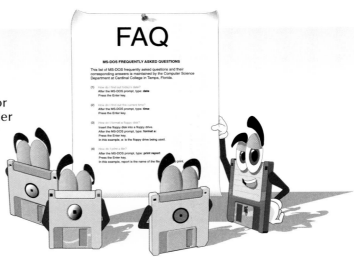

Copyright Considerations

If you are going to use information or an image from another source, make sure the information or image is not copyrighted.

Many pages on the Web offer information and images that are free from copyright restrictions.

Use Footnotes

Use footnotes to support your main documents. Footnotes can include glossaries or diagrams that help to explain your main documents. Try to keep your footnotes short and to the point.

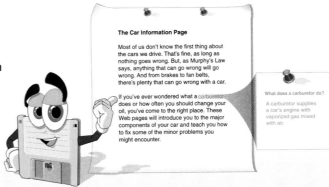

Put Useful Content on Each Page

Always include information that is valuable to the reader on each page. Even if you are designing a Web page that consists only of a table of contents, try to put some useful information on the page. This will give readers a reason to return to the Web page time and time again.

Provide General Information

Even if your Web pages are aimed at a specific audience, you should provide general background information. This ensures that any visitor to your Web pages will be able to fully understand the content of the pages you have published.

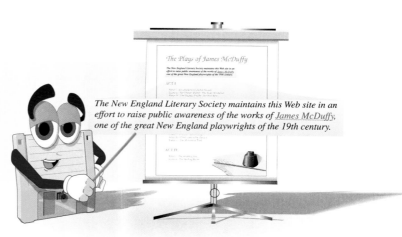

The New England Literary Society maintains this Web site in an effort to raise public awareness of the works of James McDuffy, one of the great New England playwrights of the 19th century.

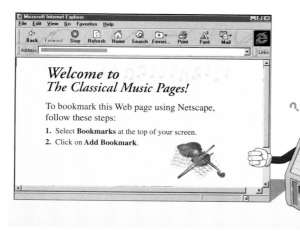

Avoid Specific Instructions

Avoid giving detailed instructions on how to perform tasks using a specific browser. People on the Web use many different browsers, and the way of performing a task may be different for each browser.

Use Warnings

If you display information that could be considered offensive by some readers, place a warning on your first Web page.

When readers visit your collection of Web pages, they will see the warning first and can then decide whether they want to read the remainder of your pages.

Proofread

Carefully check the spelling and grammar in your Web pages. A spelling mistake will make readers think that you are careless and your Web pages are inaccurate. Print out your Web pages on paper and then proofread them thoroughly.

Update Information

Change and update your Web pages on a regular basis. If the information in your Web pages never changes, people will only read the pages once and will not revisit them in the future.

> Good organization is very important for creating great Web pages. A well-organized collection of Web pages is easy to read and will attract readers time and time again.

Put Important Information First

Always display the most important information at the top of each Web page. Some readers will not scroll through a document. These readers will miss important information if it is not displayed at the top.

Emphasize Important Information

If some parts of your Web page are more important than others, use the available tools, such as headings and formatting, to make the information stand out. Do not bury important ideas or concepts in long paragraphs.

Page Length

Web pages should not be too short or too long. If a Web page is shorter than half a screen of information, try to combine the information with another page.

If a Web page is longer than five screens, readers may lose interest. You should try to break up long Web pages into several shorter pages.

Use Paragraphs

Always use paragraphs to divide the text on your Web pages into shorter sections. Most people find short paragraphs easier to read than long paragraphs.

Use Headings

Always use headings to indicate your main topics or ideas. Headings make it easier for readers to glance through a Web page and find specific information without having to read through all the content.

Condense Information

If your Web pages contain a lot of information, you can create another Web page that contains all the information from all your pages. This provides an efficient way for readers to save or print your information without having to browse through multiple Web pages.

Use Emphasis Only Where Needed

If you emphasize too many words and phrases in your Web pages, the important information will not stand out. Only emphasize words and phrases that are very important.

Use a Signature

Always put your name and e-mail address at the end of each Web page you create. This allows readers to contact you if they have any questions or comments. Also include the date to let readers know when the page was last modified.

Avoid "Under Construction" Labels

Many Web page designers display "under construction" labels on their Web pages. If some of your Web pages are not ready, do not make the pages available on the Web. It is frustrating for readers to go to a page that contains no useful information.

Images

Some people turn off the display of images in order to browse more quickly, while others use browsers that cannot display images. Always design your Web pages so that readers who do not see images will still get valuable information from your pages.

Modem Speed

Many people use slow modems to access the Web. When designing your Web pages, try to keep the combined size of the images and the Web pages as small as possible. This will speed the display of pages by reducing the time it takes for the information to transfer.

The home page is the main page in a collection of Web pages. The home page is usually the first page people read.

The home page is usually named **index.htm** or **index.html**

Use a Summary

Always place a brief summary of your Web pages on the home page. You should state whether the purpose of the Web pages is to amuse or inform readers. Never assume that readers will understand what your Web pages are about just by reading the title.

Table of Contents

Outline the contents of your Web pages on the home page. This allows readers to quickly find the information they want without having to read pages that do not interest them.

Remind Readers to Bookmark

Bookmarks are a Web browser feature that allows readers to mark Web pages for later reference. Most readers forget to use this feature, particularly if they are absorbed in reading the information on a page.

Include an image or phrase to remind readers to bookmark your page. The bookmarks feature is also called a hotlist or favorites feature.

Include a Help Section

If you have a large collection of Web pages, you should include a help section on the home page. In the help section, explain which icons or navigational tools you will use on your Web pages.

Display Design Credits

If you are creating Web pages for other people, ask if you can put your name and e-mail address at the bottom of the home page. This will let readers know how to contact you if they have questions about the design or layout of the pages.

Once you know the information that each of your Web pages will contain, you can plan the layout of your Web pages.

There are four different types of layouts you can use. You determine which layout you will need based on the type of information your Web pages contain and the way the pages relate to each other.

Linear

A linear layout organizes Web pages in a straight line. This layout works well for Web pages that should be read in a specific order, such as stories or step-by-step instructions. This type of layout is also called a slide show layout.

Each Web page typically contains links that allow readers to move back and forth through the pages. Each page may also include a link back to the home page.

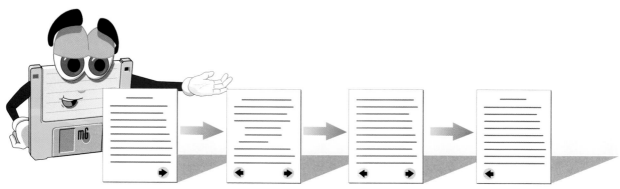

Hierarchical

In a hierarchical layout, all Web pages branch off a main page that usually contains a table of contents or index. The main Web page provides the most general information, while the additional pages provide more specific information.

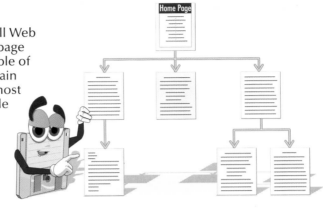

Web

A Web layout has no overall structure. This type of layout is ideal for Web pages that do not need to be read in a specific order. Readers can easily drift from one Web page to another. Web pages can include a link back to the home page or a map to help readers navigate through the pages.

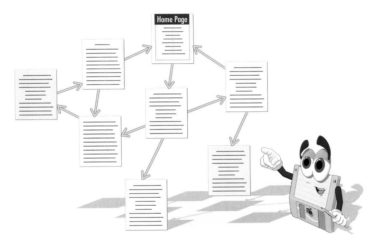

Combination

A combination of layouts provides readers with the greatest amount of flexibility when reading your Web pages. For example, using both a hierarchical and a Web layout makes it easy for readers to browse through every page or just view pages of interest.

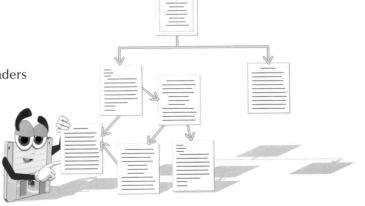

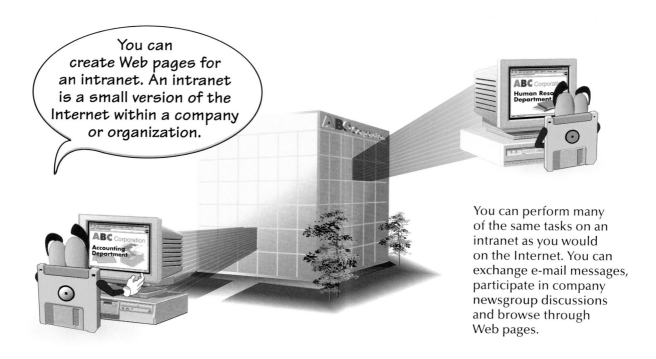

You can create Web pages for an intranet. An intranet is a small version of the Internet within a company or organization.

You can perform many of the same tasks on an intranet as you would on the Internet. You can exchange e-mail messages, participate in company newsgroup discussions and browse through Web pages.

Set Up an Intranet

An intranet is very easy to set up since most companies already have a network that connects computers to share information. You can easily turn a network into an intranet by adding a Web server to store Web pages.

Create Web Pages

Company employees can create documents and place them on the intranet for everyone to view. Most software applications have special programs that can convert existing documents into Web pages. Many new word processors and spreadsheet programs have this feature built-in.

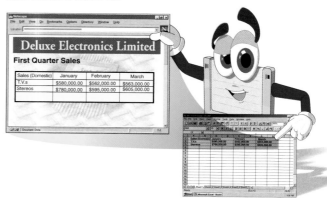

CREATE WEB PAGES FOR AN INTRANET

Share Documents

Document sharing is one of the main reasons a company or organization would set up an intranet.

You can place documents that you would not display on the Internet, such as workplace procedures or a company newsletter, on an intranet.

Include Sound and Video

Information transfers more quickly over an intranet than over the Internet. This means you can include sound and video in Web pages that would take too long to transfer over the Internet.

Update Software

A company can use an intranet to let employees easily get software programs.

When a person in the organization needs to update or install a new software program, they can transfer the software from the intranet instead of having to use floppy disks or CD-ROM discs.

CHAPTER 3

BASIC HTML

INTRODUCTION TO HTML

HyperText Markup Language (HTML) is a computer language used to create Web pages.

HTML was developed from a more powerful and elaborate computer language called Standard Generalized Markup Language (SGML).

HTML DOCUMENTS

Documents viewed on the Web are HTML documents. An HTML document consists of only text—the main text of the document and special instructions, called tags. Each tag gives a specific instruction and is surrounded by angle brackets < >.

An HTML document created using Unix or a Macintosh computer has the .html extension (example: index.html). An HTML document created using MS-DOS or Windows has the .htm extension (example: index.htm).

A Web browser interprets the tags in an HTML document and displays the document on the screen.

HTML ADVANTAGES

Transfers Quickly

Since HTML documents contain only text, these documents transfer quickly over the Web.

Displays on Any Computer

An HTML document can be displayed on any type of computer, such as a Macintosh or IBM-compatible computer. This means you only need to create one HTML document that everyone on the Web can view.

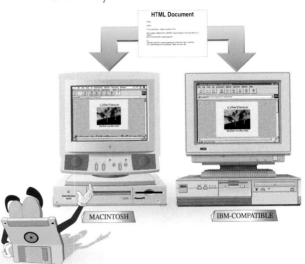

HTML VERSIONS

There are several versions of HTML. Each new version offers new tags to give authors more control when designing Web pages. All Web browsers can use the tags defined in the current HTML standard, version 2.0.

Many Web browsers already use tags proposed for the next version of HTML, version 3.2, even though this version has not yet been finalized.

Some companies that make Web browsers, such as Netscape and Microsoft, have developed their own tags. Other browsers may not be able to display these tags. If a browser does not understand a tag, the tag is ignored.

INTRODUCTION TO HTML

Document Structure

Document structure tags let you set up the basic structure of your Web pages.

Formatting

Formatting tags let you change the appearance of text.

Links

Link tags allow readers to select highlighted text or an image on your Web pages to instantly go to other Web pages.

Images

Image tags allow you to add images to your Web pages.

VIEW HTML TAGS

When browsing through the Web, you may find a page you really like. You can use your Web browser to view the HTML tags the author used to create the page. This is a great way to get ideas for improving your own Web pages.

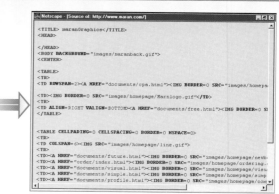

WORK WITH TAGS

Work in Pairs

Most tags have an opening tag and a closing tag that affect the text between the tags. The closing tag has a forward slash (/). Some tags have only an opening tag.

Attributes

Some tags have attributes to offer options for the tag. For example, the <FONT> tag has a COLOR attribute that lets you change the color of text in your document.

Case Insensitive

You can use uppercase or lowercase letters when typing tags. Most people type tags in uppercase letters to make the tags stand out from the main text.

Define Document Structure

The tags in an HTML document tell a Web browser about the structure of a document, but do not specifically define how to display the document. Each Web browser may interpret the HTML tags differently, so the same HTML document may not look the same in all Web browsers.

CREATE HTML DOCUMENTS

There are several types of programs you can use to create HTML documents.

You do not need a connection to the Internet to create an HTML document.

TEXT EDITOR

A text editor is a program used to create and edit documents that contain only text.

Text editors do not have the advanced editing features found in word processors.

Popular text editors include Notepad for Windows and SimpleText for the Macintosh.

In a text editor, you type the text for your document and then add HTML tags to define how you want the text to appear when viewed on the Web.

You must know exactly which tags you want to enter and make sure you place the tags in the correct locations.

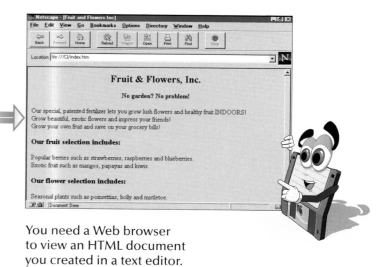

You need a Web browser to view an HTML document you created in a text editor.

WORD PROCESSOR

A word processor is a program that gives you control over the content and structure of documents you create.

A word processor has powerful editing tools, such as a search and replace feature, spell checker, grammar checker and thesaurus.

In a word processor, any formatting you apply to text will not appear when you view the document on the Web. You must use HTML tags to format text in documents you create. You must know exactly which tags you want to enter and make sure you place the tags in the correct locations.

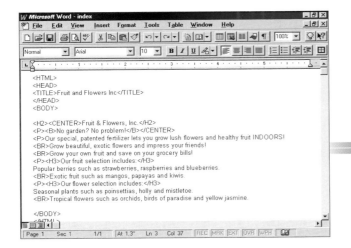

Popular word processors include Microsoft Word and Corel WordPerfect.

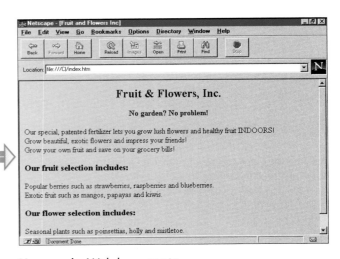

You need a Web browser to view an HTML document you created in a word processor.

CREATE HTML DOCUMENTS

HTML EDITOR

An HTML editor provides a visual way of creating Web pages. You can instantly see how a change you make will affect the Web page.

Enters Tags for You

When you select pictures or menu commands in an HTML editor, the editor enters tags into the document for you. This means that you do not have to memorize tags or know how to properly place tags in a document.

Some HTML editors display the tags in the document. Other HTML editors hide the tags and display the document as it will appear on the Web.

Offers Less Control

An HTML editor may not use some of the newer or non-standard HTML tags. As a result, HTML editors generally offer you less control over your documents.

Popular HTML Editors

You can get trial versions of these popular
HTML editors from the following Web sites:

Netscape Navigator Gold
http://home.netscape.com

Microsoft FrontPage
http://www.microsoft.com

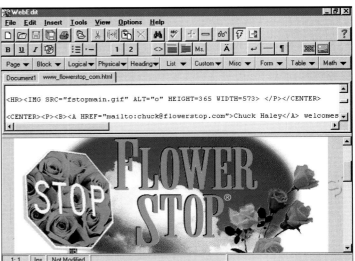

Kenn Nesbitt's WebEdit
http://www.nesbitt.com

You can easily create Web pages by using a word processor or text editor.

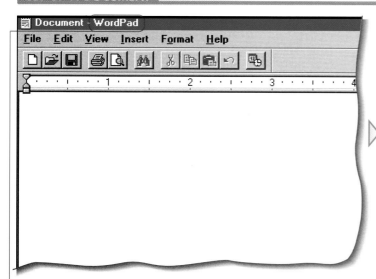

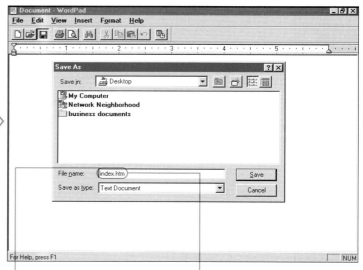

1 Start the word processor or text editor you will use to create the document.

2 Save and name the document as a text file. The document name can be eight characters long and consist of letters and numbers, but no spaces. The main document in a collection of Web pages is usually called **index**.

Make sure you add an extension to the document name. Type **.htm** if you are using MS-DOS or Windows. Type **.html** if you are using Unix or a Macintosh computer.

Should I be concerned when the text scrolls off my screen?

When you type a long paragraph in a text editor or simple word processor, the text may scroll off the edge of the screen. However, when you view the document in a Web browser, the text will fit properly on the screen.

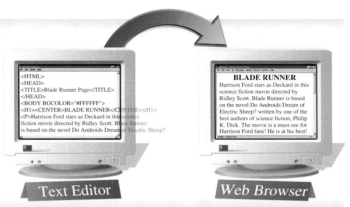

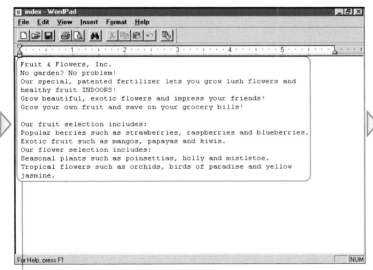

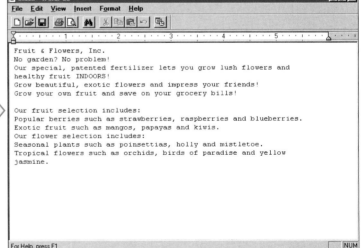

3 Type the text you want to appear on the Web page.

■ Make sure you frequently save the document to store any changes you make.

4 Check the document for spelling and grammar errors.

■ Do not format the text in the document. You must use HTML tags to format the text.

There are some basic tags you must add to every HTML document you create.

You need to identify the document as an HTML document.

The head contains information about the document, such as the title.

HTML

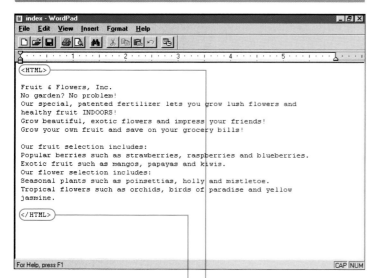

```
<HTML>

Fruit & Flowers, Inc.
No garden? No problem!
Our special, patented fertilizer lets you grow lush flowers and
healthy fruit INDOORS!
Grow beautiful, exotic flowers and impress your friends!
Grow your own fruit and save on your grocery bills!

Our fruit selection includes:
Popular berries such as strawberries, raspberries and blueberries.
Exotic fruit such as mangos, papayas and kiwis.
Our flower selection includes:
Seasonal plants such as poinsettias, holly and mistletoe.
Tropical flowers such as orchids, birds of paradise and yellow
jasmine.

</HTML>
```

Although many browsers can display a document without the HTML tags, it is considered proper form to include these tags in a document.

1 Type **<HTML>** before all the text in the document.

2 Type **</HTML>** after all the text in the document.

HEAD

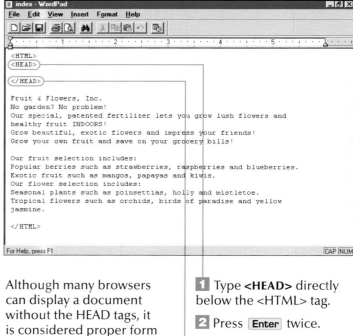

```
<HTML>
<HEAD>

</HEAD>

Fruit & Flowers, Inc.
No garden? No problem!
Our special, patented fertilizer lets you grow lush flowers and
healthy fruit INDOORS!
Grow beautiful, exotic flowers and impress your friends!
Grow your own fruit and save on your grocery bills!

Our fruit selection includes:
Popular berries such as strawberries, raspberries and blueberries.
Exotic fruit such as mangos, papayas and kiwis.
Our flower selection includes:
Seasonal plants such as poinsettias, holly and mistletoe.
Tropical flowers such as orchids, birds of paradise and yellow
jasmine.

</HTML>
```

Although many browsers can display a document without the HEAD tags, it is considered proper form to include these tags in a document.

1 Type **<HEAD>** directly below the <HTML> tag.

2 Press **Enter** twice.

3 Type **</HEAD>**

You must give the document a title that describes its contents. The title usually appears in the title bar of a window.

The body contains the contents of the document.

TITLE

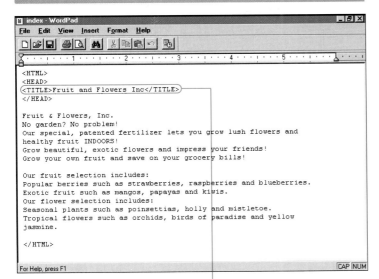

A title should be brief and descriptive and should interest people in reading the Web page. Use titles like "Advanced Golf Techniques" rather than less descriptive titles such as "Chapter Two" or "My Home Page."

1 Type **<TITLE>** directly below the <HEAD> tag.

2 Type the title of the Web page, using only letters and numbers (A to Z and 0 to 9).

3 Type **</TITLE>**

BODY

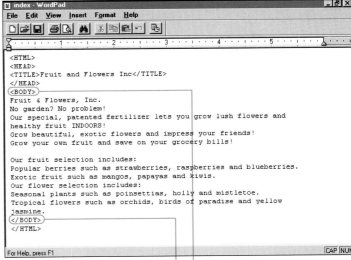

You must place the BODY tags around the contents of the document.

1 Type **<BODY>** directly below the </HEAD> tag.

2 Type **</BODY>** directly above the </HTML> tag.

You can use your Web browser to view an HTML document you created. This lets you see how other people on the Web will view your document.

VIEW A DOCUMENT IN BROWSER

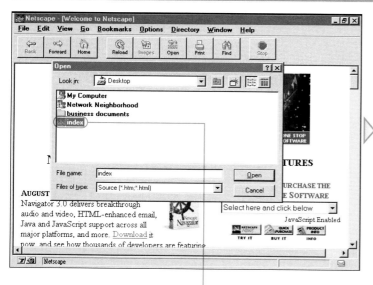

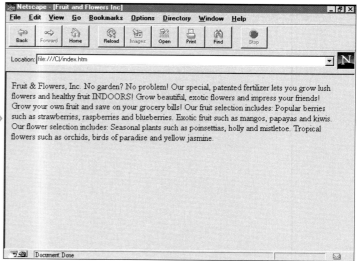

1 Start your Web browser.

2 Open your HTML document in the Web browser window. In this example, the index.htm file will be opened.

■ The document appears in the Web browser window.

Can anyone else see my document?

Even though you can view the document in your Web browser, other people on the Web cannot view the document.

You must transfer the document to a company that makes pages available on the Web before other people can view the document.

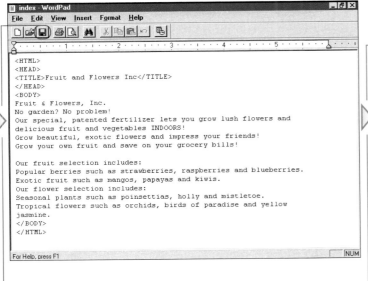

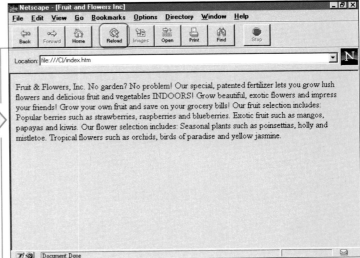

VIEW CHANGES

1 After you make changes to the HTML document, save the changes.

2 To view the changes, reload, or refresh, the document in the Web browser window.

START A NEW PARAGRAPH

When creating an HTML document, you must use tags to specify where you want each paragraph to begin.

NANCY'S MOVIE REVIEWS

Visit this site to find out my opinions of the latest movies!

Voices from Space

\<P\> Thrilling special effects and outstanding acting performances make Voices from Space one of the best movies of the year.

\<P\> Victor Carling stars as Thomas Nelson, a veteran NASA astronaut aboard a gigantic space station orbiting Mars in the year 2045. The station's long-range sensors begin to detect mysterious signals, and the station's crew members must decide what actions to take.

\<P\> Carling's performance propels Stephen Reid's thoughtful screenplay to incredible heights of intensity and excitement. Impressive performances are also given by Sheila Tyler and Gordon White, who co-star as crew members aboard the station.

START A NEW PARAGRAPH

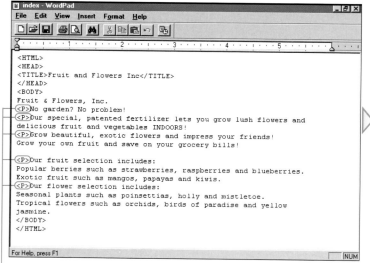

1 Type **\<P\>** in front of each paragraph in your document.

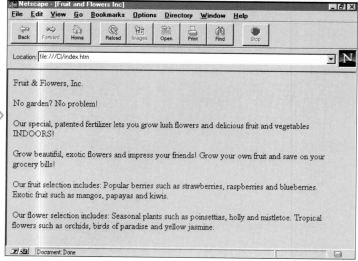

■ The Web browser displays a blank line between each paragraph.

START A NEW LINE

When creating an HTML document, you must use tags to specify where you want each new line of text to begin.

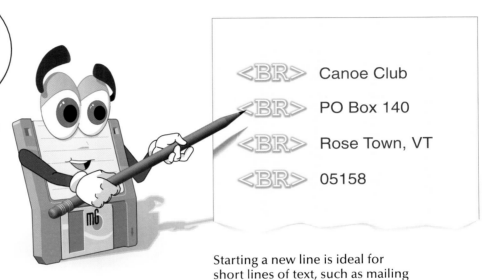

 Canoe Club

 PO Box 140

 Rose Town, VT

 05158

Starting a new line is ideal for short lines of text, such as mailing addresses or lines of poetry.

START A NEW LINE

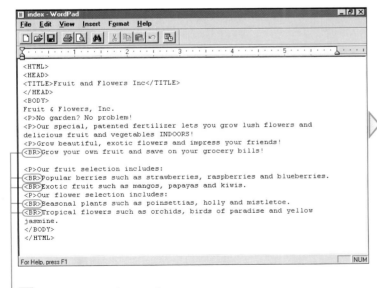

1 Type **
** in front of each phrase you want to appear on its own line.

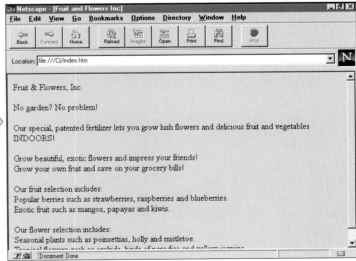

■ The Web browser displays each phrase on its own line.

PREFORMATTED TEXT

A Web browser usually ignores any new lines, paragraphs and extra spaces you place in an HTML document. You can retain the appearance of a section of text by using tags.

Preformatted text is useful for lining up information in a table.

DELUXE ELECTRONICS LIMITED
(First Quarter)

Income Statement

	January	February	March	Total
REVENUE	8700	11500	13670	33870
Payroll	3850	4850	5250	13950
Rent	1750	1750	1750	5250
Supplies	1920	1980	2030	5930
TOTAL	7520	8580	9030	25130
INCOME	1180	2920	4640	8740

PREFORMATTED TEXT

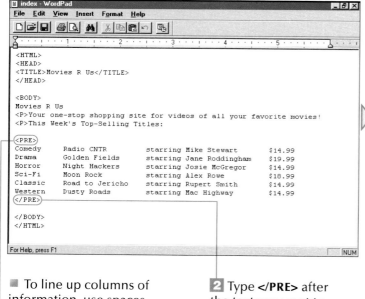

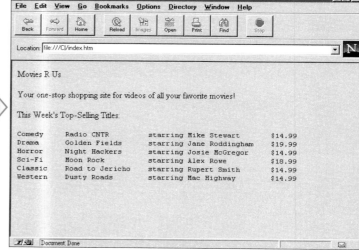

■ To line up columns of information, use spaces, not tabs.

1 Type **<PRE>** in front of the text you want to preformat.

2 Type **</PRE>** after the text you want to preformat.

■ The Web browser displays the text using the exact spacing you used in the HTML document.

ADD A HEADING

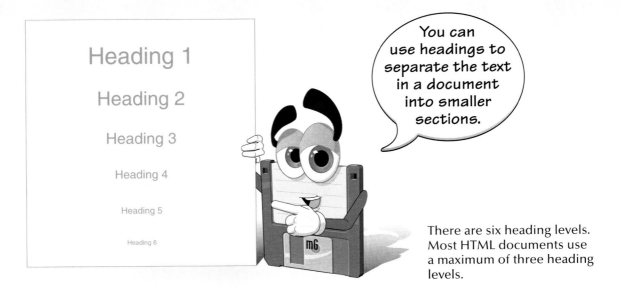

You can use headings to separate the text in a document into smaller sections.

There are six heading levels. Most HTML documents use a maximum of three heading levels.

ADD A HEADING

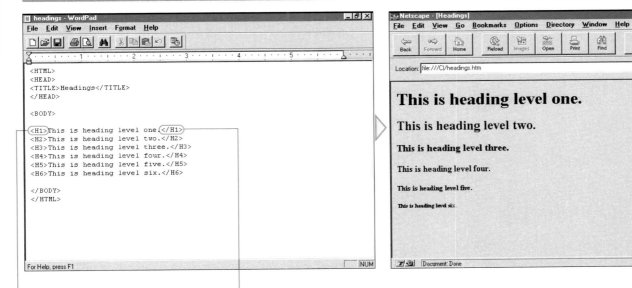

1 Type **<H?>** in front of the text you want to make a heading. Replace **?** with a number from 1 to 6 (example: <H1>).

2 Type **</H?>** after the heading. Replace **?** with the number you selected in step **1**.

■ The Web browser displays the headings.

Heading Levels

Levels 1, 2 and 3 are often used for document and section titles.

Level 4 is the same size as the main text in a document.

Levels 5 and 6 are often used for copyright or disclaimer information.

Subheadings

When creating subheadings, do not skip heading levels. For example, an H2 heading should be followed by an H3 subheading.

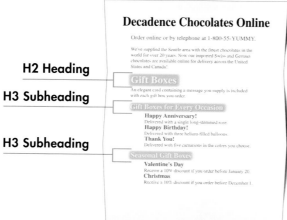

H2 Heading

H3 Subheading

H3 Subheading

Repeat the Title

The first heading in a document should repeat the document title or present a shorter version of the title. This helps readers quickly determine the overall content of a Web page. This heading will also appear at the top of the page if a reader decides to print the document.

Provide an Outline

You can use headings to provide an outline of the document for your readers. By scanning the headings, a reader should get a general overview of the information covered in the document and be able to quickly locate topics of interest.

Use Headings Consistently

Make sure you use headings consistently to help readers understand the relative importance of information in the document. Use the same heading level for all headings of equal importance.

Proper Use of Headings

Use headings to signify the importance of information in your document. Do not use headings to add a certain look or style to text. Since different Web browsers display headings in different ways, you cannot predict exactly how a heading will look to readers.

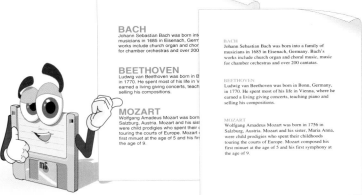

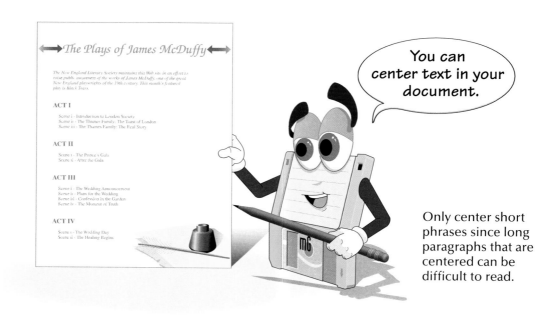

You can center text in your document.

Only center short phrases since long paragraphs that are centered can be difficult to read.

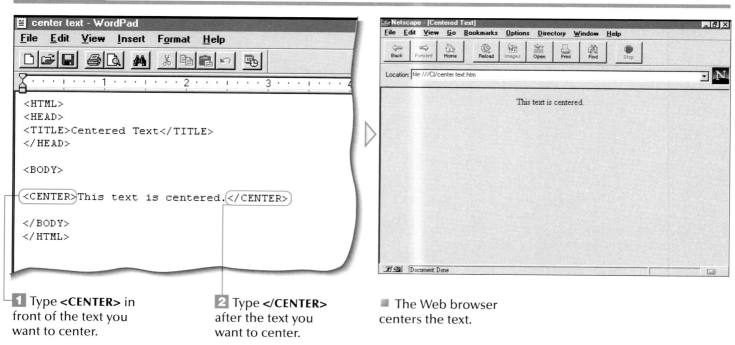

1 Type **<CENTER>** in front of the text you want to center.

2 Type **</CENTER>** after the text you want to center.

■ The Web browser centers the text.

You can align text in three different ways.

ALIGN TEXT

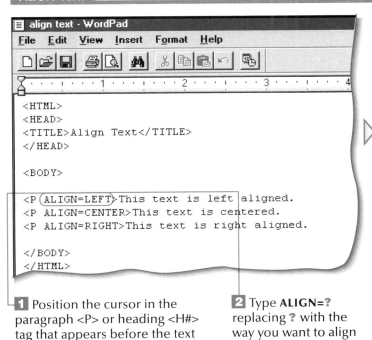

```
<HTML>
<HEAD>
<TITLE>Align Text</TITLE>
</HEAD>

<BODY>

<P ALIGN=LEFT>This text is left aligned.
<P ALIGN=CENTER>This text is centered.
<P ALIGN=RIGHT>This text is right aligned.

</BODY>
</HTML>
```

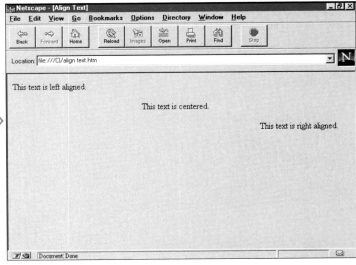

1 Position the cursor in the paragraph <P> or heading <H#> tag that appears before the text you want to align differently.

2 Type **ALIGN=?** replacing **?** with the way you want to align the text (example: ALIGN=LEFT).

■ The Web browser displays the text with the alignment you selected.

INSERT SPECIAL CHARACTERS

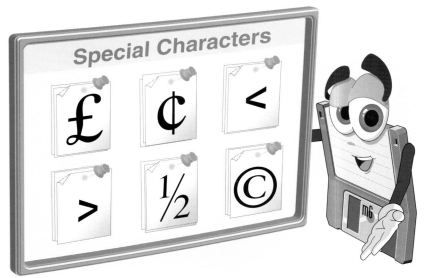

You can add characters to your Web pages that do not appear on your keyboard.

If you want to include characters that are reserved for creating HTML documents, such as <, >, " or &, you must also perform the steps below.

INSERT SPECIAL CHARACTERS

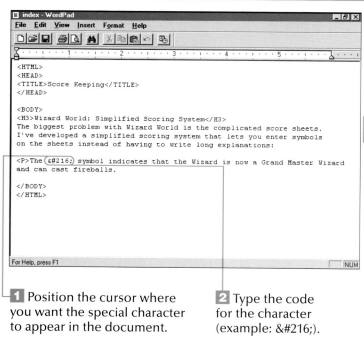

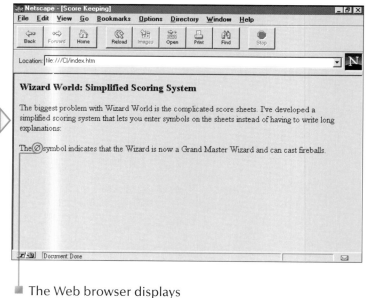

1 Position the cursor where you want the special character to appear in the document.

2 Type the code for the character (example: Ø).

■ The Web browser displays the special character.

CODE	MAC	PC		CODE	MAC	PC		CODE	MAC	PC
"	"	"		»	»	»		ß	ß	ß
&	&	&		¼	π	¼		à	à	à
/	/	/		½	Π	½		á	á	á
;	;	;		¾	≤	¾		â	â	â
<	<	<		¿	¿	¿		ã	ã	ã
>	>	>		À	À	À		ä	ä	ä
@	@	@		Á	Á	Á		å	å	å
^	^	^		Â	Â	Â		æ	æ	æ
`	`	`		Ã	Ã	Ã		ç	ç	ç
~	~	~		Ä	Ä	Ä		è	è	è
¡	¡	¡		Å	Å	Å		é	é	é
¢	¢	¢		Æ	Æ	Æ		ê	ê	ê
£	£	£		Ç	Ç	Ç		ë	ë	ë
¤	¤	¤		È	È	È		ì	ì	ì
¥	¥	¥		É	É	É		í	í	í
¦	¦	¦		Ê	Ê	Ê		î	î	î
§	§	§		Ë	Ë	Ë		ï	ï	ï
¨	¨	¨		Ì	Ì	Ì		ð	›	ð
©	©	©		Í	Í	Í		ñ	ñ	ñ
ª	ª	ª		Î	Î	Î		ò	ò	ò
«	«	«		Ï	Ï	Ï		ó	ó	ó
¬	¬	¬		Ð	<	Ð		ô	ô	ô
­	–	-		Ñ	Ñ	Ñ		õ	õ	õ
®	®	®		Ò	Ò	Ò		ö	ö	ö
¯	-	—		Ó	Ó	Ó		÷	÷	÷
°	°	°		Ô	Ô	Ô		ø	ø	ø
±	±	±		Õ	Õ	Õ		ù	ù	ù
²	2	2		Ö	Ö	Ö		ú	ú	ú
³	3	3		×	x	x		û	û	û
´	´	´		Ø	Ø	Ø		ü	ü	ü
µ	µ	µ		Ù	Ù	Ù		ý	‡	ý
¶	¶	¶		Ú	Ú	Ú		þ	fl	þ
·	·	·		Û	Û	Û		ÿ	ÿ	ÿ
¸	¸	¸		Ü	Ü	Ü				
¹	¹	¹		Ý	†	Ý				
º	º	º		Þ	fi	Þ				

The way special characters look in a Web browser depends on the browser being used and which browser font has been selected.

As a result, a person viewing your Web page may see a different character than you intended.

Want to add style to your Web pages? In this chapter you will learn how to use some additional HTML features.

Movies R Us

Your one-stop shopping site for videos of all your favorite movies! We ship around the world!

TODAY'S FEATURED SELECTION:
Space Monster, Part 7: The Director's Cut

This Week's Top-Selling Titles:

Comedy	Radio CNTR	~~$19.99~~	**$14.99**
Drama	Golden Fields	~~$24.99~~	**$19.99**
Horror	Night Hackers	~~$19.99~~	**$14.99**
Science Fiction	Moon Rock	~~$22.99~~	**$18.99**
The Classics	Road to Jericho	~~$17.99~~	**$14.99**
Western	Dusty Roads	~~$18.99~~	**$14.99**

About our company.
Cool jobs at Movies R Us: Now Hiring!
Complete our customer survey and win great prizes!

Copyright © 1996 Movies R Us. All rights reserved.

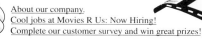

MORE HTML

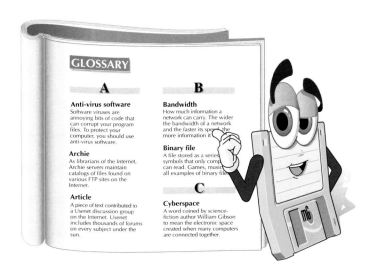

You can emphasize text on your Web page by bolding or italicizing the text.

bold *italic*

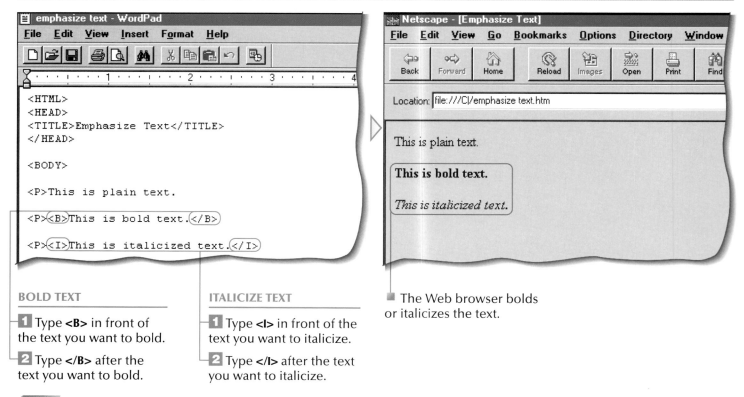

BOLD TEXT

1 Type **<B>** in front of the text you want to bold.

2 Type **</B>** after the text you want to bold.

ITALICIZE TEXT

1 Type **<I>** in front of the text you want to italicize.

2 Type **</I>** after the text you want to italicize.

■ The Web browser bolds or italicizes the text.

You can place a line through text on your Web page. This is useful when you want to show changes to information.

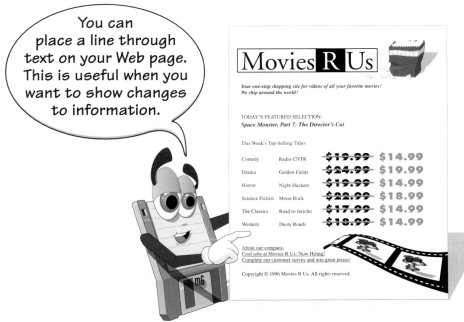

Companies often strike out old prices to show that new prices are lower.

STRIKE OUT TEXT

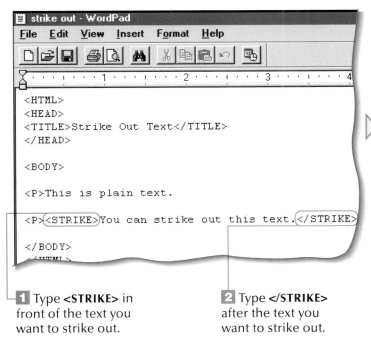

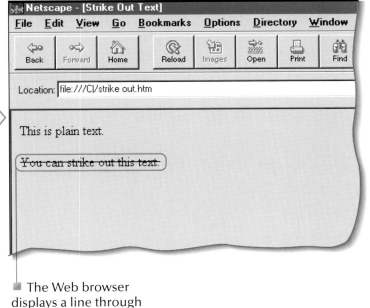

1 Type **<STRIKE>** in front of the text you want to strike out.

2 Type **</STRIKE>** after the text you want to strike out.

■ The Web browser displays a line through the text.

You can make text look like it was produced by a typewriter.

Typewriter text is often used to show commands the reader can enter into a computer.

TYPEWRITER TEXT

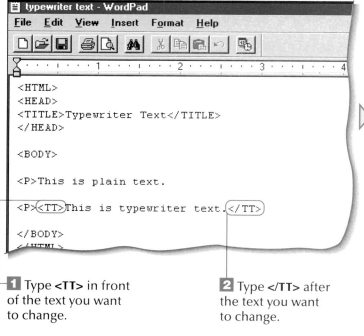

1 Type **<TT>** in front of the text you want to change.

2 Type **</TT>** after the text you want to change.

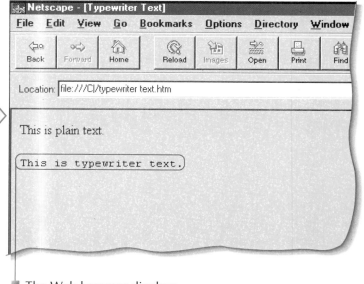

■ The Web browser displays the text as if the text was typed on a typewriter.

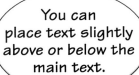

You can place text slightly above or below the main text.

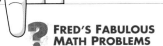

? FRED'S FABULOUS MATH PROBLEMS

Are you a high school student who needs extra practice solving math problems? If so, then you've come to the right place. My name is Fred Carter & I'm a retired math teacher living in Florida. Every Monday, I present a new set of math questions.

This Week's Problems:

(1) $X^2 * X^3 = 243$

(2) $X_0 * X_1 - X_2 = 86$

(3) $X^2 - y = 31$

SUPERSCRIPT OR SUBSCRIPT TEXT

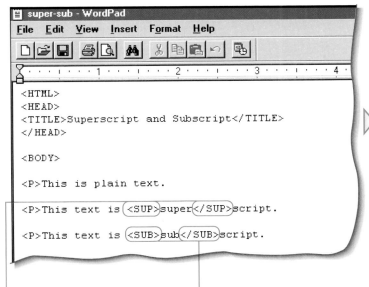

```
<HTML>
<HEAD>
<TITLE>Superscript and Subscript</TITLE>
</HEAD>

<BODY>

<P>This is plain text.

<P>This text is <SUP>super</SUP>script.

<P>This text is <SUB>sub</SUB>script.
```

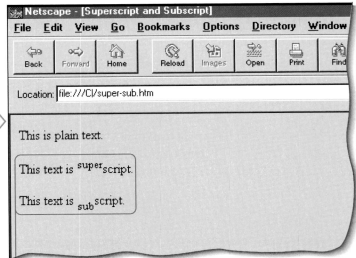

This is plain text.

This text is ^{super}script.

This text is $_{sub}$script.

SUPERSCRIPT TEXT

1 Type **<SUP>** in front of the text you want to superscript.

2 Type **</SUP>** after the text you want to superscript.

SUBSCRIPT TEXT

1 Type **<SUB>** in front of the text you want to subscript.

2 Type **</SUB>** after the text you want to subscript.

■ The Web browser displays the text slightly above or below the main text.

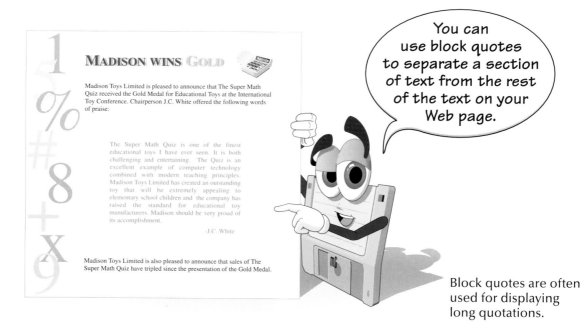

You can use block quotes to separate a section of text from the rest of the text on your Web page.

Block quotes are often used for displaying long quotations.

BLOCK QUOTES

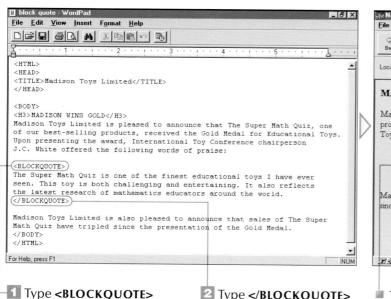

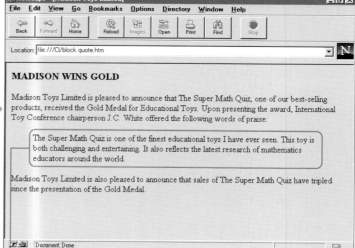

1 Type **<BLOCKQUOTE>** in front of the text you want to display as a block quote.

2 Type **</BLOCKQUOTE>** after the text you want to display as a block quote.

■ The Web browser separates the text from the rest of the document.

You can add a comment that readers will not see when they view your Web page.

You can use comments to remind you to update a section of text or to indicate why you used a specific tag.

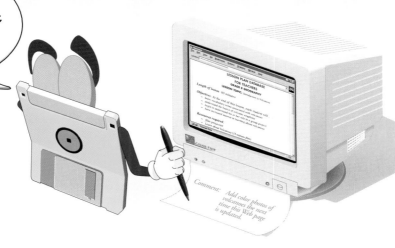

Comment: Add color photos of volumes the next time this Web page is updated.

ADD A COMMENT

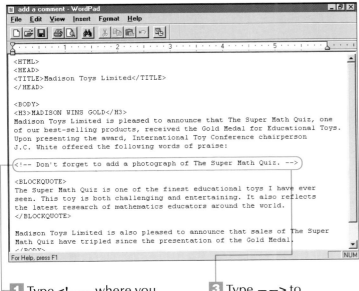

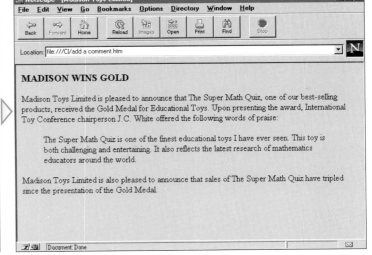

1 Type **<!––** where you want to insert a comment. Then press the **Spacebar** to add a blank space.

2 Type the comment. Then press the **Spacebar** to add another blank space.

3 Type **––>** to complete the comment.

■ The Web browser does not display your comment.

■ When adding comments, remember that people on the Web will be able to read the comments if they view the HTML document you used to create the Web page.

CHANGE FONT SIZE

You can change the size of text in part or all of your Web page.

A larger font size makes information easier to read. A smaller font size lets you fit more information on a single screen.

CHANGE SECTION OF TEXT

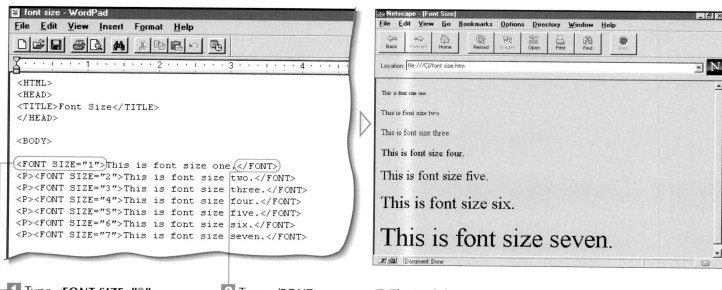

1 Type **<FONT SIZE="?">** in front of the text you want to change. Replace **?** with a number from 1 to 7. The smallest font size is 1; the largest font size is 7.

2 Type **</FONT>** after the text you want to change.

■ The Web browser displays the text at the new size.

How can I add special text effects to my Web pages?

You can change the size of characters in your document to create many interesting text effects.

CHANGE ENTIRE DOCUMENT

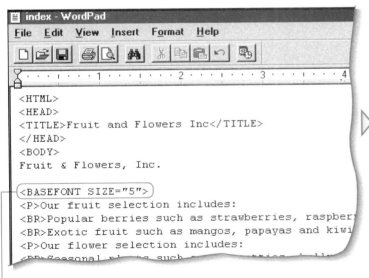

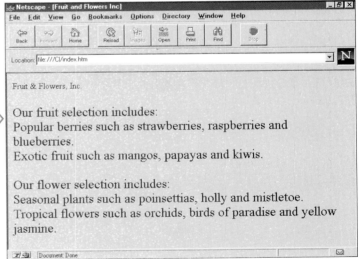

1 Type **<BASEFONT SIZE="?">** in front of the text you want to change. Replace **?** with a number from 1 to 7. The smallest font size is 1; the largest font size is 7.

■ The Web browser displays all the text following the <BASEFONT SIZE> tag at the new size.

■ The <BASEFONT SIZE> tag will not affect the size of headings in your document. For information on headings, refer to pages 61-63.

You can change the color of text in part or all of your Web page.

Most pages on the Web display black text.

CHANGE SECTION OF TEXT

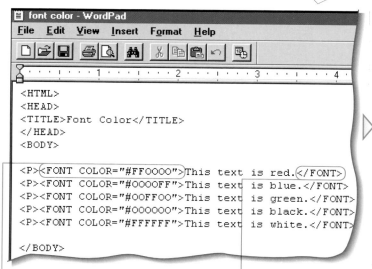

```
<HTML>
<HEAD>
<TITLE>Font Color</TITLE>
</HEAD>
<BODY>

<P><FONT COLOR="#FF0000">This text is red.</FONT>
<P><FONT COLOR="#0000FF">This text is blue.</FONT>
<P><FONT COLOR="#00FF00">This text is green.</FONT>
<P><FONT COLOR="#000000">This text is black.</FONT>
<P><FONT COLOR="#FFFFFF">This text is white.</FONT>

</BODY>
```

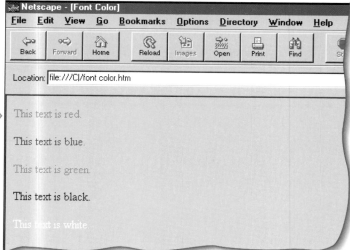

This text is red.

This text is blue.

This text is green.

This text is black.

This text is white.

1 Type **<FONT COLOR="?">** in front of the text you want to change. Replace **?** with the code for the color you want to use (example: <FONT COLOR="#FF0000">).

2 Type **</FONT>** after the text you want to change.

■ The Web browser displays the text in the color you selected.

What are some commonly used colors on the Web?

These are some of the most commonly used colors on the Web. You can get a more complete list of colors at the maranGraphics Web site:

http://www.maran.com/colorchart

Black	#OOOOOO
Blue	#OOOOFF
Gray	#CCCCCC
Green	#OOFFOO
Red	#FFOOOO
White	#FFFFFF

CHANGE ENTIRE DOCUMENT

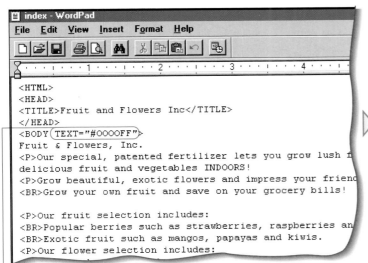

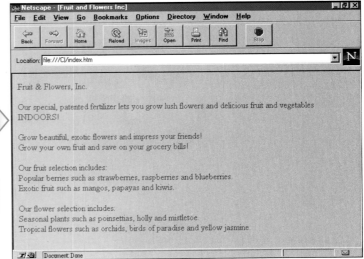

1 In the <BODY> tag, type **TEXT="?"** replacing **?** with the code for the color you want to use (example: TEXT="#OOOOFF").

■ The Web browser displays all the text in the color you selected.

CHANGE BACKGROUND COLOR

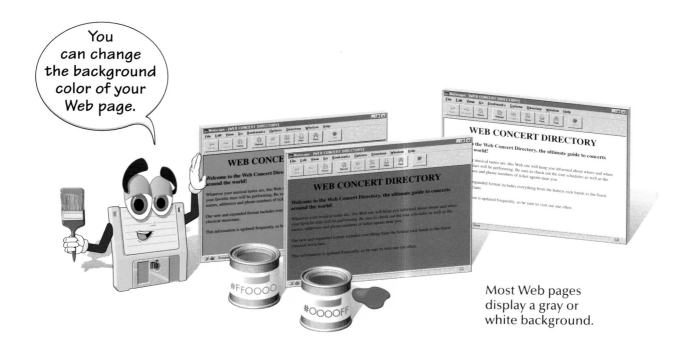

You can change the background color of your Web page.

Most Web pages display a gray or white background.

CHANGE BACKGROUND COLOR

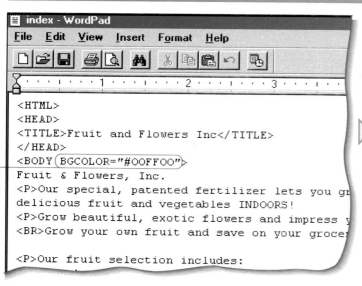

1 In the <BODY> tag, type **BGCOLOR="?"** replacing **?** with the code for the color you want to use (example: BGCOLOR="#OOFFOO").

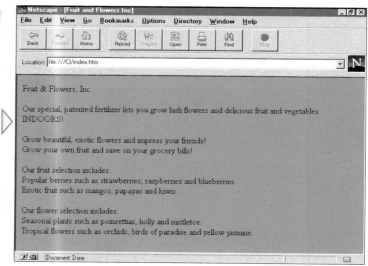

■ The Web browser displays the background color you selected.

Common Colors

These are some of the most commonly used colors on the Web. You can get a more complete list of colors at the maranGraphics Web site:

http://www.maran.com/colorchart

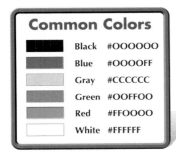

Common Colors

■	Black	#OOOOOO
■	Blue	#OOOOFF
■	Gray	#CCCCCC
■	Green	#OOFFOO
■	Red	#FFOOOO
□	White	#FFFFFF

Contrast

Make sure you select text colors and background colors that work well together. For example, red text on a blue background can be difficult to read.

Individual Preference

Web browsers can be set to override the colors defined for a Web page. This allows readers to display all Web pages with the colors they prefer. This means that the colors you choose for your Web page may not appear the way you expect on some computers.

Color Blindness

When adding color to your document, consider that millions of people are color blind. The most common form of color blindness is the inability to distinguish between red and green.

An ordered list consists of items in a specific order. An ordered list is ideal for a set of instructions or a table of contents.

Aunt Ida's Banana Nut Bread

1. Cream together butter and sugar.
2. Sift flour, soda and salt.
3. Add nuts and mashed bananas

You can add additional items to an ordered list. The Web browser will automatically renumber the items in the list.

CREATE AN ORDERED LIST

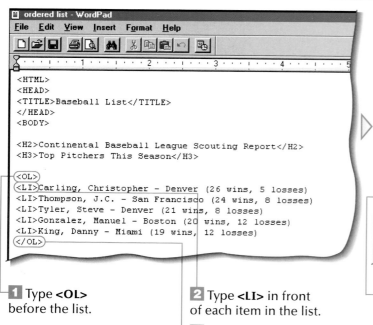

```
<HTML>
<HEAD>
<TITLE>Baseball List</TITLE>
</HEAD>
<BODY>

<H2>Continental Baseball League Scouting Report</H2>
<H3>Top Pitchers This Season</H3>

<OL>
<LI>Carling, Christopher - Denver (26 wins, 5 losses)
<LI>Thompson, J.C. - San Francisco (24 wins, 8 losses)
<LI>Tyler, Steve - Denver (21 wins, 8 losses)
<LI>Gonzalez, Manuel - Boston (20 wins, 12 losses)
<LI>King, Danny - Miami (19 wins, 12 losses)
</OL>
```

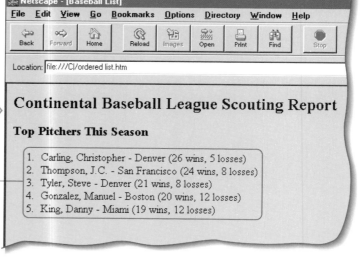

Continental Baseball League Scouting Report

Top Pitchers This Season

1. Carling, Christopher - Denver (26 wins, 5 losses)
2. Thompson, J.C. - San Francisco (24 wins, 8 losses)
3. Tyler, Steve - Denver (21 wins, 8 losses)
4. Gonzalez, Manuel - Boston (20 wins, 12 losses)
5. King, Danny - Miami (19 wins, 12 losses)

1 Type **<OL>** before the list.

2 Type **<LI>** in front of each item in the list.

3 Type **</OL>** after the list.

■ The Web browser displays the list.

What number styles can I use to number a list?

You can use one of the following number styles in your list.

NUMBER STYLE	RESULT
A	A,B,C
a	a,b,c
I	I,II,III
i	i,ii,iii
1	1,2,3

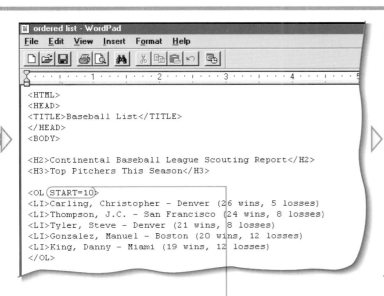

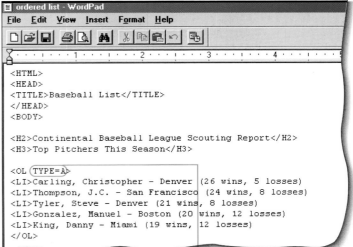

CHANGE STARTING NUMBER

Ordered lists automatically start with the number 1. You can start the list with a different number.

1 In the <OL> tag, type **START=?** replacing **?** with the number you want to use to start the list (example: START=10).

CHANGE NUMBER STYLE

Ordered lists automatically use Arabic numerals (1, 2, 3). You can use a different number style in the list.

1 In the <OL> tag, type **TYPE=?** replacing **?** with the number style you want to use (example: TYPE=A). For a list of number styles, see above.

> An unordered list consists of items in no particular order, such as a list of products.

Pasta *Perfection*

- Order our specialty pasta online for fast delivery.
- Browse through our recipe files.

Our Most Popular Types of Pasta:

- **Cannelloni**
- **Lasagna**
- **Linguine**
- **Manicotti**
- **Ravioli**
- **Spaghetti**

Perfect pasta every time!

CREATE AN UNORDERED LIST

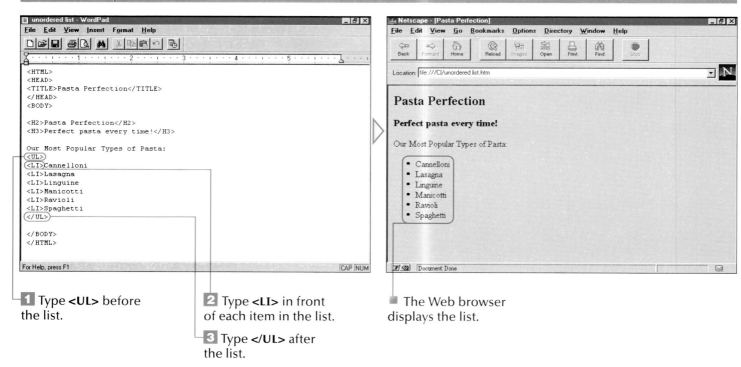

1 Type **<UL>** before the list.

2 Type **<LI>** in front of each item in the list.

3 Type **</UL>** after the list.

■ The Web browser displays the list.

A definition list consists of terms and their definitions. This type of list is ideal for a glossary.

CREATE A DEFINITION LIST

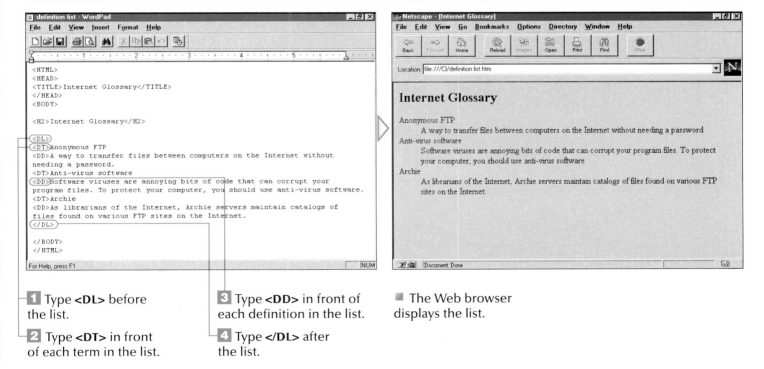

1 Type **<DL>** before the list.

2 Type **<DT>** in front of each term in the list.

3 Type **<DD>** in front of each definition in the list.

4 Type **</DL>** after the list.

■ The Web browser displays the list.

CHAPTER 5
IMAGES

There are many ways you can use images on your Web pages. Images can make your pages more inviting and interesting.

Art

A Web page can display drawings, paintings or computer-generated art. Many people display their favorite paintings or art created by their children or themselves.

Graphic design companies often display art on their Web pages to advertise their work.

Photographs

You can include photographs of your family, pets or favorite celebrities to share with people all over the world.

Many companies include photographs of products on their Web pages. This lets people around the world view the products without having to visit the store or wait for a brochure to arrive in the mail.

Background Images

You can create an interesting background design or texture by repeating a small image to fill an entire Web page.

Explanations

An image can help clarify a concept that is difficult to explain with words. You can include a map to give directions, a chart to show financial trends or a diagram to point out essential parts of a product.

Dividing Lines

You can use images as dividing lines to visually separate different sections of a Web page.

Dividing lines indicate where one section ends and another begins. This helps readers quickly find topics of interest.

Navigational Tools

You can use images as navigational tools to help readers browse through your Web pages.

A reader can select an image to move back and forth through your Web pages.

There are many ways you can get images to place on your Web pages.

Clip Art

Clip art is an inexpensive collection of ready-made images that you can buy at most computer stores. There are clip art collections of cartoons, drawings, photographs and computer-generated art. Make sure images you buy are in a format that can be viewed on the Web (GIF or JPEG). For information on GIF and JPEG, refer to page 100.

Scanned Images

You can use a scanner to read images into a computer. You can scan photographs, logos and drawings and then place the scanned images on your Web pages.

Make sure you ask for permission before using images you scan from published work such as a magazine or book. If you do not have a scanner, there are many service bureaus that will scan images for a fee.

Internet

There are many places on the Internet that offer images you can use on your Web pages. Make sure you have permission to use any images you copy from the Internet.

You can get images at the following Web sites:

http://www.erinet.com/cunning1/tiles.html

http://www.users.interport.net/~traff/graphics

http://www.cli.di.unipi.it:80/iconbrowser

Create Images

You can use a paint program to create your own images. Creating your own images gives you the most control and lets you design images that best suit your Web pages. Paint programs also let you modify existing images and create interesting text effects.

You can buy professional paint programs, such as Adobe Photoshop and Corel Photo-Paint, at computer stores. There are also less complex paint programs you can get on the Internet.

Paint Shop Pro (Windows)

http://www.jasc.com

ShareDraw (Macintosh)

http://www.peircesw.com/ShareDraw.html

Be Selective

Carefully examine each image you want to include and decide whether or not each image is really needed. Only include images that serve a useful function.

Randomly placing unnecessary images in a document may make the document seem cluttered and disorganized.

View Web Pages Without Images

Make sure your Web pages will make sense and look attractive without any images. Some readers turn off the display of images to browse more quickly, while others use browsers that cannot display images.

You can offer a text alternative for readers who do not see images on their screen.

Refer to Images

You can organize images used on your Web pages by storing all the images in one directory.

When you want to refer to an image stored in the same directory as your Web pages, type the name of the image (example: castle.gif).

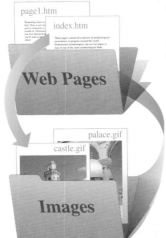

When you want to refer to an image stored in a subdirectory, type the name of the subdirectory followed by the name of the image (example: images/castle.gif).

Transfer Speeds

Images increase the time it takes for a Web page to appear on a screen. Most readers will wait about 10 to 15 seconds to view a Web page. If a page takes a longer period of time to appear, readers may lose interest and skip to another page.

Whenever possible, use small images rather than large images, since large images take longer to transfer. Keep the total size of your HTML document and all images under 150 K (kilobytes).

Copyright

You may find images in books, newspapers, magazines or on the Internet that you want to use in your Web pages. Make sure you have permission before placing any copied images in your Web pages.

Large Images

If you want to include a large image on a Web page, consider creating a smaller version of the image that links to the larger version. This lets readers decide if they want to wait to view the larger version.

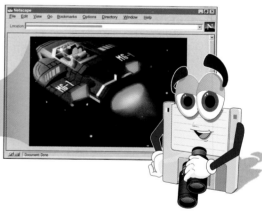

Reusing Images

A single image can appear on a Web page several times without significantly increasing the transfer time. When a reader displays a Web page, the computer temporarily stores the images. When the same image appears on a Web page more than once, the computer displays a copy of the stored image.

Image Resolution

The resolution of an image refers to the quality of the image. Higher resolution images are sharper and more detailed. Most monitors display images at 72 dots per inch (dpi).

Unless you want readers to print your images, images do not need to have resolutions higher than 72 dpi. Higher resolutions unnecessarily increase the size of the image file.

Image Width

Make sure any images on your Web pages are less than 480 pixels wide. An image wider than 480 pixels may not fit on the screen.

Text-Only Version

Some readers turn off the display of images, while others use browsers that cannot display images. If your Web pages contain a lot of images, you can create a text-only version specifically designed for these readers.

A text-only version will also help visually impaired readers, since the color and size of text can quickly be changed.

ADD A HORIZONTAL RULE

You can place lines across your Web page to visually separate sections of the page.

ADD A HORIZONTAL RULE

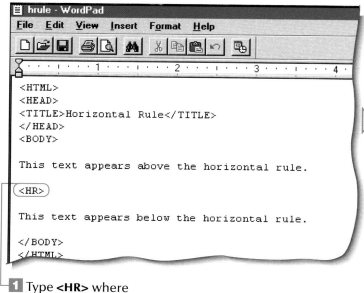

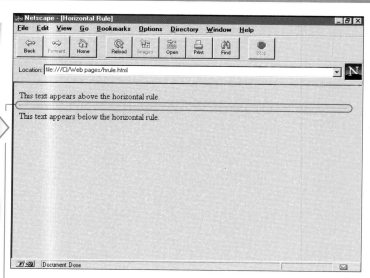

1 Type **<HR>** where you want to insert a horizontal rule.

■ The Web browser displays the horizontal rule.

Thickness

No Shade

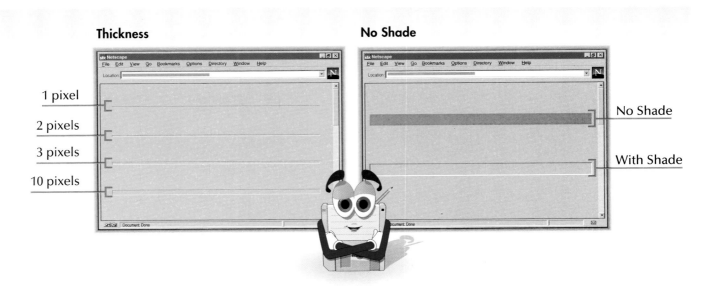

1 pixel

2 pixels

3 pixels

10 pixels

No Shade

With Shade

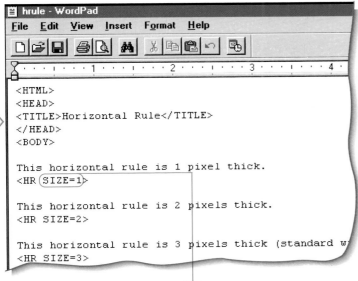

CHANGE THICKNESS

You can change
the thickness of a
horizontal rule.

1 In the <HR> tag, type
SIZE=? replacing **?** with
the thickness you want
to use for the horizontal
rule in pixels.

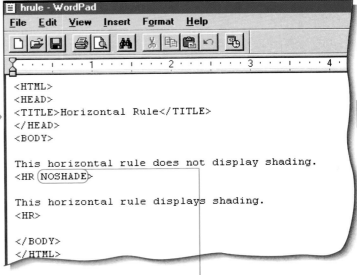

NO SHADE

You can change a
three-dimensional
horizontal rule to a
flat, two-dimensional
rule by removing the
shading.

1 In the <HR> tag,
type **NOSHADE**

CONT🤖NUED➡

ADD A HORIZONTAL RULE

You can change the width of a horizontal rule if you do not want the rule to extend across the entire document.

When you change the width of a horizontal rule, the rule will appear centered on your Web page. You can easily change the alignment of the rule.

ADD A HORIZONTAL RULE (CONTINUED)

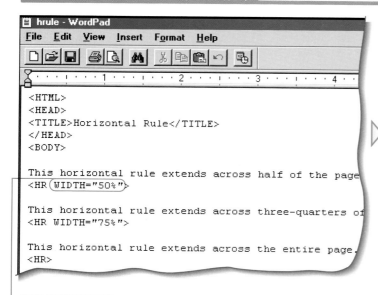

```
hrule - WordPad
File  Edit  View  Insert  Format  Help

<HTML>
<HEAD>
<TITLE>Horizontal Rule</TITLE>
</HEAD>
<BODY>

This horizontal rule extends across half of the page
<HR WIDTH="50%">

This horizontal rule extends across three-quarters of
<HR WIDTH="75%">

This horizontal rule extends across the entire page.
<HR>
```

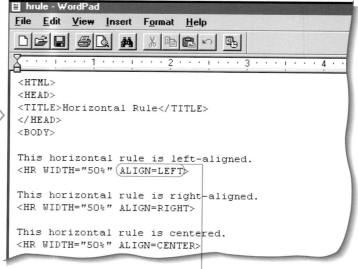

```
hrule - WordPad
File  Edit  View  Insert  Format  Help

<HTML>
<HEAD>
<TITLE>Horizontal Rule</TITLE>
</HEAD>
<BODY>

This horizontal rule is left-aligned.
<HR WIDTH="50%" ALIGN=LEFT>

This horizontal rule is right-aligned.
<HR WIDTH="50%" ALIGN=RIGHT>

This horizontal rule is centered.
<HR WIDTH="50%" ALIGN=CENTER>
```

CHANGE WIDTH

1 In the <HR> tag, type **WIDTH="?%"** replacing **?** with the percentage of the document you want the horizontal rule to extend across.

CHANGE ALIGNMENT

After changing the width of a horizontal rule, you can change its alignment.

1 In the <HR> tag, type **ALIGN=?** replacing **?** with the way you want to align the horizontal rule (example: ALIGN=LEFT).

Separate Main Document

You can use horizontal rules to separate the main document from the header and footer. The header often includes a title or table of contents. The footer often includes author and document information.

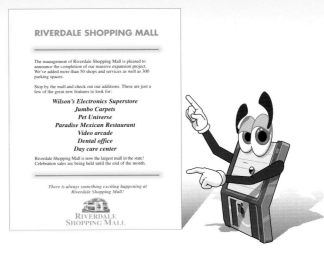

Do Not Overuse

Do not overuse horizontal rules in your Web pages, since this can annoy readers. Try not to place more than one horizontal rule on each screen.

Use Images

You can use images instead of lines to visually separate sections of a document. You can create your own horizontal rule images in a paint program or get images from the Internet.

The following Web sites offer images you can use as horizontal rules:

http://www.benber.com/dividers.htm

http://www.gla.ac.uk/Clubs/WebSoc/graphics/lines

http://www.idb.hist.no/~geirme/gizmos/lines/lines.html

GIF

Graphics Interchange Format (GIF) images are the most common type of image found on the Web. GIF images are limited to 256 colors, which is the same number of colors most computer monitors can display. GIF is often used for logos, banners and computer-generated art. GIF images have the .gif extension.

JPEG

Joint Photographic Experts Group (JPEG) images are commonly found on the Web. JPEG images can have millions of colors and are often used for photographs and very complex images. JPEG images have the .jpg, .jpe or .jpeg extension.

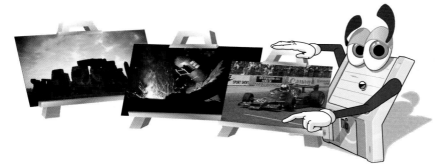

PNG

Portable Network Graphics (PNG) images are a newer type of image specifically designed for use on the Web. PNG images can have millions of colors and will eventually replace GIF images. PNG images have the .png or .ping extension.

CONVERT TO GIF OR JPEG

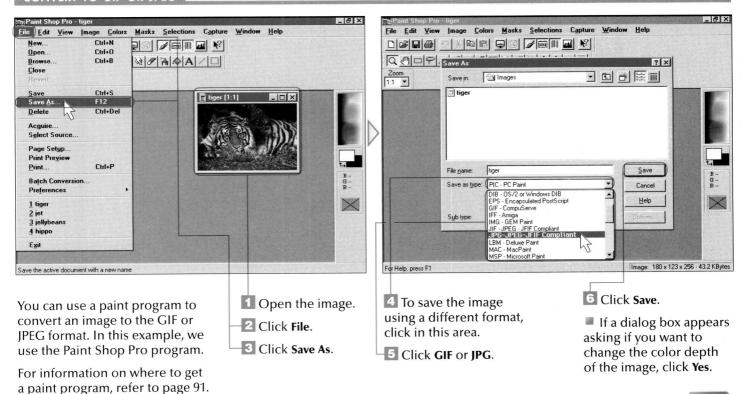

You can use a paint program to convert an image to the GIF or JPEG format. In this example, we use the Paint Shop Pro program.

For information on where to get a paint program, refer to page 91.

1 Open the image.

2 Click **File**.

3 Click **Save As**.

4 To save the image using a different format, click in this area.

5 Click **GIF** or **JPG**.

6 Click **Save**.

■ If a dialog box appears asking if you want to change the color depth of the image, click **Yes**.

ADD AN IMAGE

You can easily add an image to a Web page. An image that appears on a Web page is called an inline image.

ADD AN IMAGE

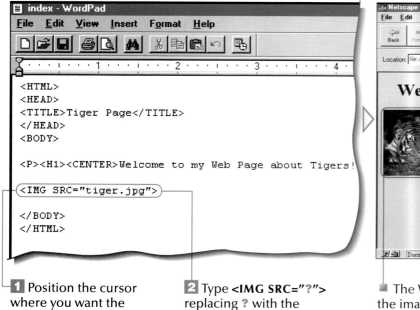

1 Position the cursor where you want the image to appear.

2 Type **<IMG SRC="?">** replacing **?** with the location of the image on your computer.

■ The Web browser displays the image on the Web page.

CENTER AN IMAGE

You can center images on your Web pages. Centered images can give your pages a more pleasing appearance.

CENTER AN IMAGE

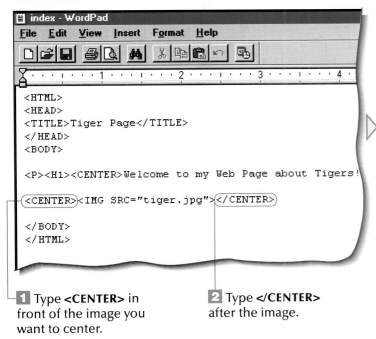

```
<HTML>
<HEAD>
<TITLE>Tiger Page</TITLE>
</HEAD>
<BODY>

<P><H1><CENTER>Welcome to my Web Page about Tigers!

<CENTER><IMG SRC="tiger.jpg"></CENTER>

</BODY>
</HTML>
```

1 Type **<CENTER>** in front of the image you want to center.

2 Type **</CENTER>** after the image.

■ The Web browser displays the image centered on the Web page.

GIVE ALTERNATIVE TEXT

Since some readers may not see the images on your Web pages, you can specify the text you want to display instead of the images. This will help these readers know what they are missing.

Some readers use Web browsers that cannot display images, while others turn off the display of images to browse more quickly.

GIVE ALTERNATIVE TEXT

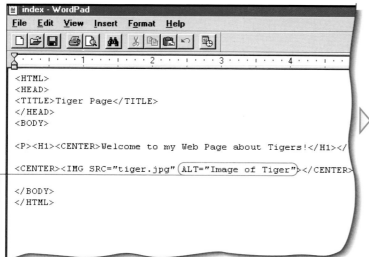

1 In the <IMG> tag, type **ALT="?"** replacing **?** with the text you want to appear if the image does not.

■ If the image does not appear, the Web browser will display the text you specified.

Note: The alternative text may not appear in place of the image until after you publish your page on the Web.

Note: Borders may not appear if you are using Microsoft Internet Explorer.

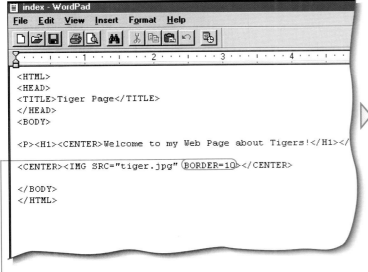

■1 In the <IMG> tag, type **BORDER=?** replacing **?** with the border thickness you want to use in pixels.

■ The Web browser displays a border around the image.

■ To remove an existing border, replace **?** with the number 0 in step ■1.

You can have a small image repeat to fill an entire Web page. This can add an interesting background texture.

ADD A BACKGROUND IMAGE

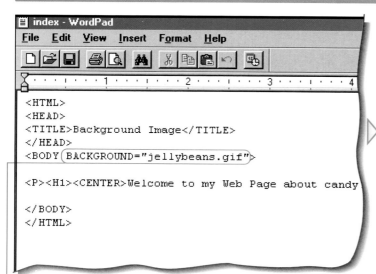

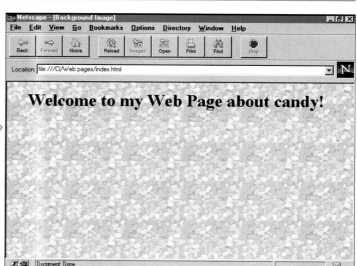

1 In the <BODY> tag, type **BACKGROUND="?"** replacing **?** with the location of the image on your computer.

■ The Web browser repeats the image to fill the entire Web page.

BACKGROUND IMAGE TIPS

Good Background Images

Choose an image that creates an interesting background design without overwhelming your Web page. Since background images increase the time it takes for a page to appear on a screen, choose a background image with a small file size.

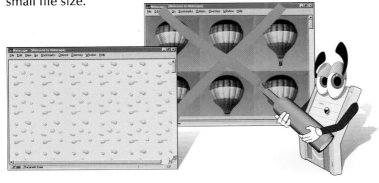

Web Page Readability

Make sure the background image you choose does not affect the readability of your Web page. You may need to change the text color to make the page easier to read.

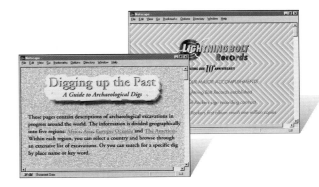

Seamless Background

A good background image should have invisible edges. When the images fill the Web page, you should not be able to tell where the edges of the images meet.

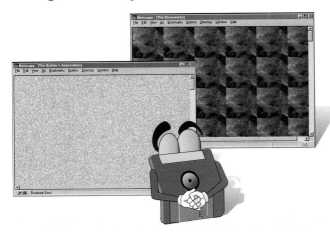

Get Background Images

You can get background images at the following Web sites:

http://www.netscape.com/assist/net_sites/bg/backgrounds.html

http://www.ECNet.Net/users/gas52r0/Jay/backgrounds/back.htm

http://www.ender-design.com/rg/backidx.html

CHAPTER **6**

MORE IMAGES

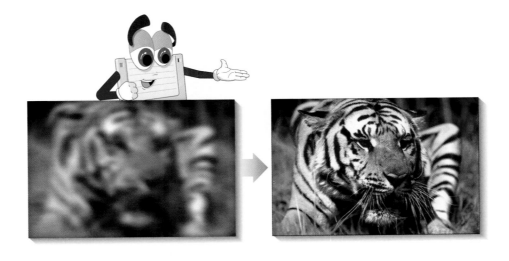

> You can define the width and height of an image. This lets the image appear more quickly since Web browsers do not have to calculate this information.

DEFINE SIZE OF IMAGE

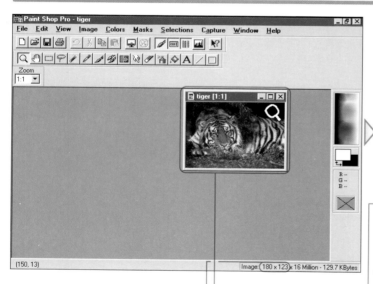

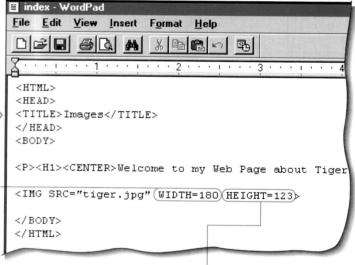

DETERMINE SIZE OF IMAGE

You can use a paint program, such as Paint Shop Pro, to determine the exact width and height of an image. For information on where to get a paint program, refer to page 91.

1 Open the image.

2 Move the mouse anywhere over the image.

■ This area displays the width and height of the image in pixels.

DEFINE SIZE OF IMAGE

1 In the <IMG> tag, type **WIDTH=?** replacing **?** with the width of the image in pixels.

2 Press the **Spacebar**. Then type **HEIGHT=?** replacing **?** with the height of the image in pixels.

CHANGE SIZE OF IMAGE

You can change the size of an image on a Web page.

Avoid making images too big since enlarged images may appear grainy.

CHANGE SIZE OF IMAGE

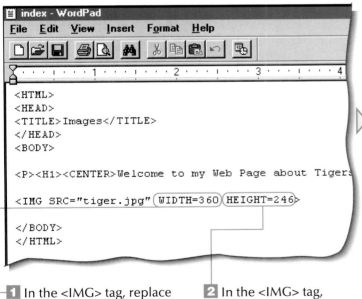

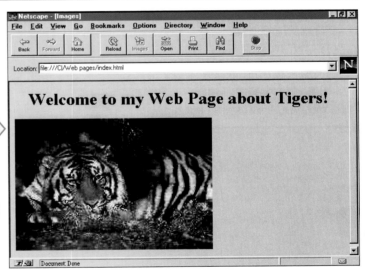

1 In the <IMG> tag, replace the WIDTH value with the width you want to use in pixels. To keep the image in proportion, make sure you use multiples of the original width and height.

2 In the <IMG> tag, replace the HEIGHT value with the height you want to use in pixels.

■ The Web browser displays the image at the new size.

WRAP TEXT AROUND IMAGE

You can have text wrap around an image. This can give your Web page a professional look.

WRAP TEXT AROUND IMAGE

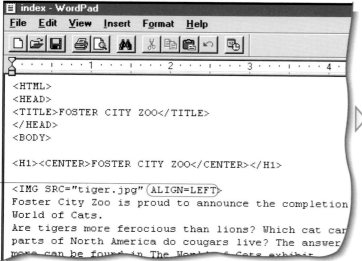

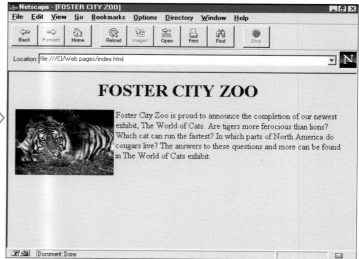

1 To place an image on the left side of a Web page and have the text wrap around the right side of the image, type **ALIGN=LEFT** in the <IMG> tag.

■ To place an image on the right side of a Web page and have the text wrap around the left side of the image, type **ALIGN=RIGHT** in the <IMG> tag.

■ The Web browser displays the text wrapped around the image.

Voices from Space

Thrilling special effects and outstanding acting performances make Voices from Space one of the best movies of the year.

Science fiction fans will love every minute of this suspense-filled masterpiece. And fans of good acting will appreciate the return of Victor Carling to the big screen. Carling stars as Thomas Nelson, a veteran NASA astronaut assigned to routine space station duty in the year 2045.

> You can stop text from wrapping around an image. The text will continue when the left, right or all margins are clear of images.

STOP TEXT WRAP

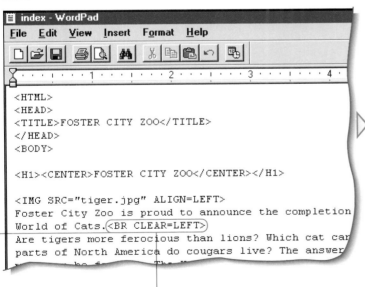

1 Position the cursor where you want the text to stop wrapping.

2 Type **<BR CLEAR=?>** replacing **?** with the margin(s) you want to be clear of images before the text continues (LEFT, RIGHT, ALL).

■ The Web browser breaks the text where you specified.

ALIGN TEXT AND IMAGE

There are three ways you can align images with text.

ALIGN TEXT AND IMAGE

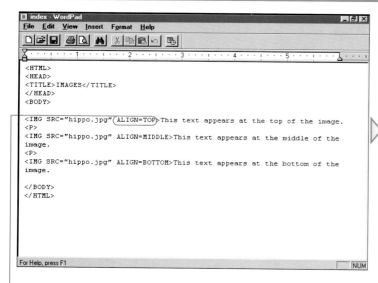

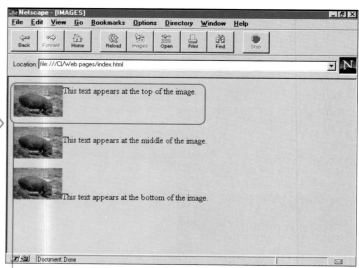

1 In the <IMG> tag, type **ALIGN=?** replacing **?** with the way you want to align the text with the image (example: ALIGN=TOP).

■ The Web browser displays the text and image with the new alignment.

You can increase the space between an image and the surrounding text.

A Web browser usually leaves 2 pixels of space around an image.

ADD SPACE AROUND IMAGE

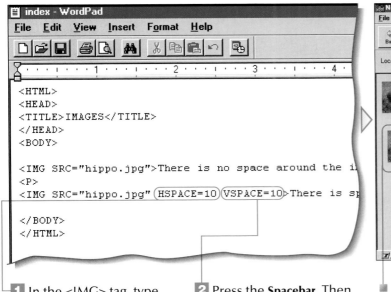

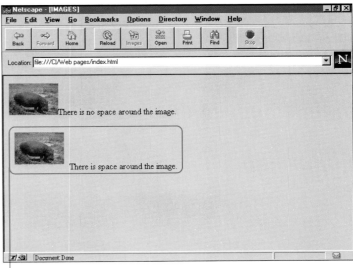

1 In the <IMG> tag, type **HSPACE=?** replacing **?** with the amount of space you want to add to the left and right sides of the image in pixels.

2 Press the **Spacebar**. Then type **VSPACE=?** replacing **?** with the amount of space you want to add above and below the image in pixels.

■ The Web browser adds space around the image.

A thumbnail image is a small version of an image that links to a larger version. Thumbnail images let readers decide if they want to wait to view the full-size image.

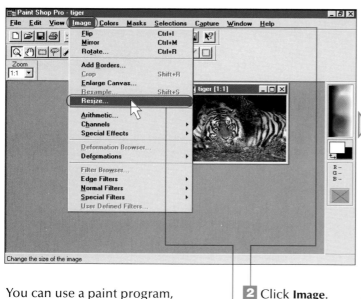

CREATE A THUMBNAIL IMAGE

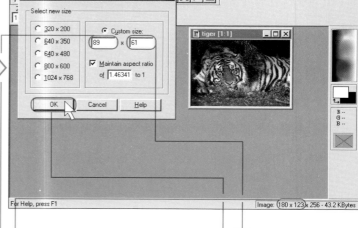

You can use a paint program, such as Paint Shop Pro, to create a thumbnail image. For information on where to get a paint program, refer to page 91.

1 Open the image.

2 Click **Image**.

3 Click **Resize**.

■ This area displays the original width and height of the image.

4 Double-click this area and then type a new width. To keep the image in proportion, reduce the width and height by a multiple of the original values.

5 Double-click this area and then type a new height.

6 Click **OK**.

What is the difference between an inline image and an external image?

An inline image is an image that appears directly on a Web page.

An external image is an image that appears only when a reader selects a link to the image. You can create a thumbnail image to link to an external image.

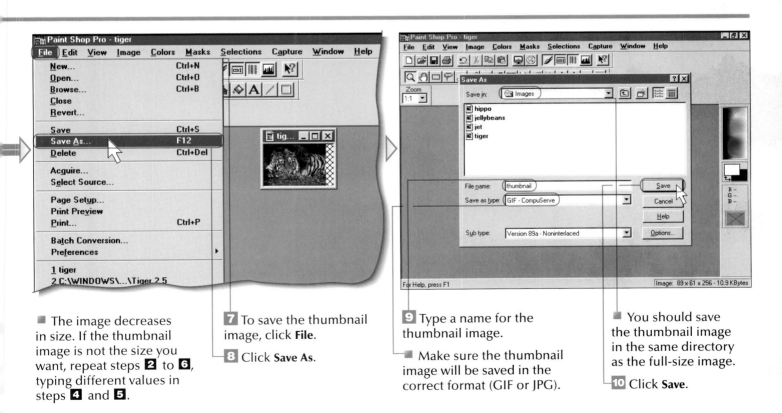

■ The image decreases in size. If the thumbnail image is not the size you want, repeat steps **2** to **6**, typing different values in steps **4** and **5**.

7 To save the thumbnail image, click **File**.

8 Click **Save As**.

9 Type a name for the thumbnail image.

■ Make sure the thumbnail image will be saved in the correct format (GIF or JPG).

■ You should save the thumbnail image in the same directory as the full-size image.

10 Click **Save**.

CREATE A THUMBNAIL IMAGE

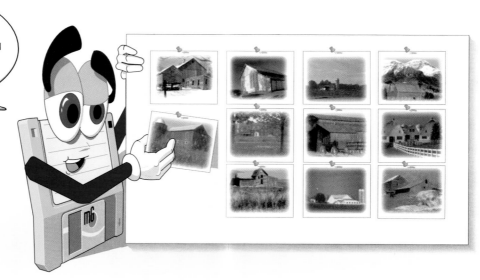

Once you have created a thumbnail image, you can place it in your Web page.

PLACE THUMBNAIL IMAGE IN WEB PAGE

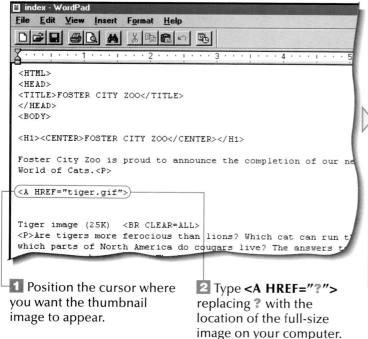

1 Position the cursor where you want the thumbnail image to appear.

2 Type **<A HREF="?">** replacing **?** with the location of the full-size image on your computer.

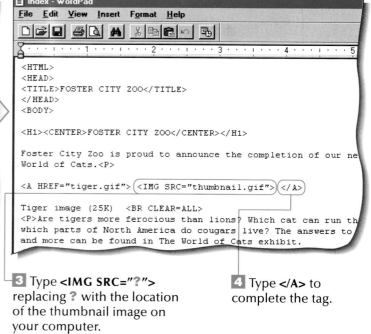

3 Type **<IMG SRC="?">** replacing **?** with the location of the thumbnail image on your computer.

4 Type **</A>** to complete the tag.

How long will the full-size image take to appear?

Many Web pages display the size of the larger image in kilobytes (K) beside the thumbnail image. This allows readers to estimate how long the full-size image will take to appear on the screen.

The Full-Size Image is 100 K

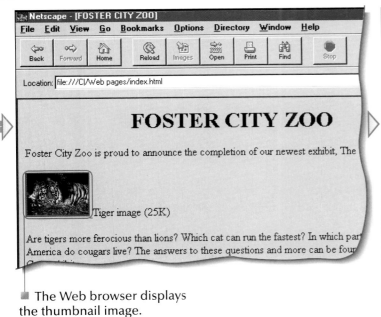

■ The Web browser displays the thumbnail image.

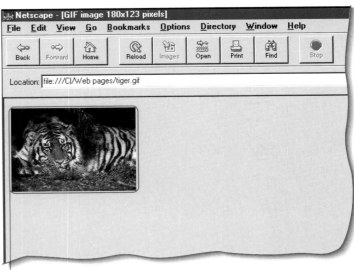

■ When a reader selects the thumbnail image, the full-size version of the image will appear.

INTERLACE GIF IMAGE

Unlike GIF images, which appear one line at a time, interlaced GIF images appear all at once. An interlaced GIF image first appears blurry, then gradually sharpens until the entire image is transferred.

Interlaced GIF images are ideal when you want to display large images on your Web pages.

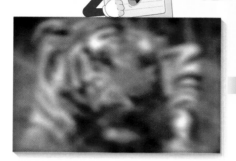 

INTERLACE GIF IMAGE

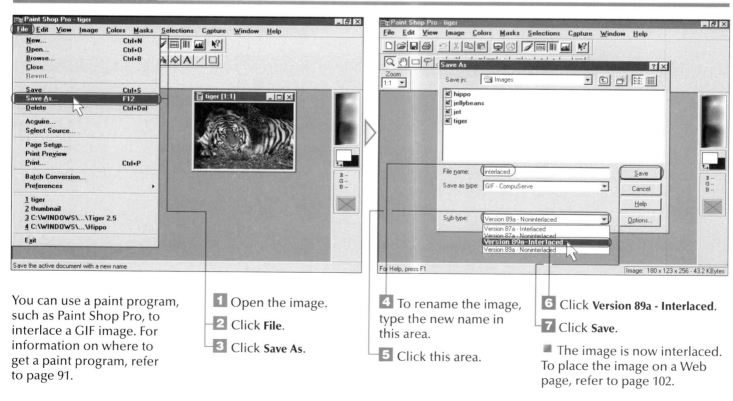

You can use a paint program, such as Paint Shop Pro, to interlace a GIF image. For information on where to get a paint program, refer to page 91.

1 Open the image.

2 Click **File**.

3 Click **Save As**.

4 To rename the image, type the new name in this area.

5 Click this area.

6 Click **Version 89a - Interlaced**.

7 Click **Save**.

■ The image is now interlaced. To place the image on a Web page, refer to page 102.

You can reduce the number of colors in an image. This will decrease the size of the image file so it can transfer more quickly over the Internet.

REDUCE COLORS IN IMAGE

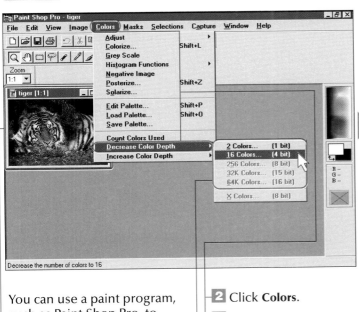

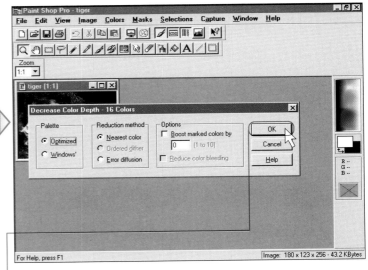

You can use a paint program, such as Paint Shop Pro, to reduce the number of colors in an image. For information on where to get a paint program, refer to page 91.

1 Open the image.

2 Click **Colors**.

3 Click **Decrease Color Depth**.

4 Click the number of colors you want the image to contain.

■ The **Decrease Color Depth** dialog box appears.

5 Click **OK**.

6 To save the changes, perform steps **2** to **4** and then step **7** on page 120.

■ The number of colors in the image is now reduced. To place the image on a Web page, refer to page 102.

You can make the background of an image invisible so the image blends into a Web page. The background of the image will remain invisible even if the background of the page changes.

TRANSPARENT GIF IMAGES

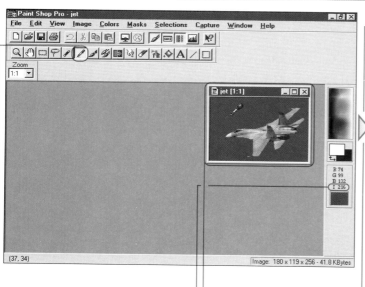

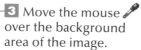

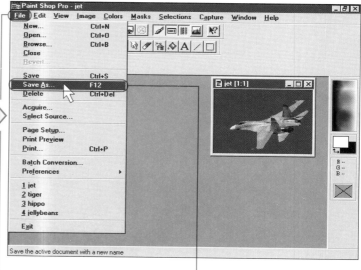

You can use a paint program, such as Paint Shop Pro, to make the background of an image transparent. For information on where to get a paint program, refer to page 91.

1 Open the image.

2 Click the dropper.

3 Move the mouse over the background area of the image.

4 Write down the Index (I) value for the background.

5 To save the image, click **File**.

6 Click **Save As**.

Single Background Color

Choose images with a single background color. If an image has a multicolored background, you must change the background to a single color before making the background transparent.

Different Background Color

Make sure the background color does not appear in the image itself. When you make the background of an image transparent, every part of the image that matches the background color will also become transparent.

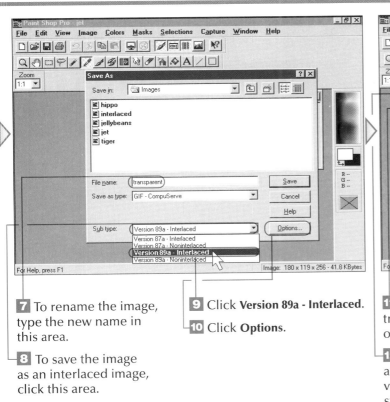

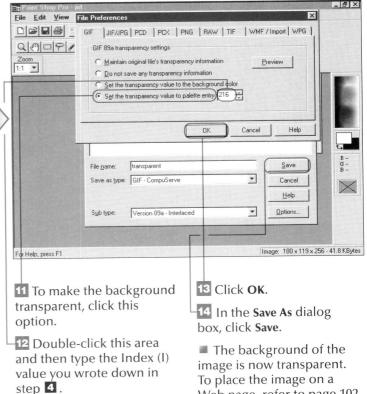

7 To rename the image, type the new name in this area.

8 To save the image as an interlaced image, click this area.

9 Click **Version 89a - Interlaced**.

10 Click **Options**.

11 To make the background transparent, click this option.

12 Double-click this area and then type the Index (I) value you wrote down in step **4**.

13 Click **OK**.

14 In the **Save As** dialog box, click **Save**.

■ The background of the image is now transparent. To place the image on a Web page, refer to page 102.

CHAPTER 7

LINKS

You can link text or images in your Web pages to related information on the Web. Linking is what makes the Web such a powerful tool.

Web pages that contain links are hypertext documents. The term hypermedia is replacing the term hypertext because the Web now also includes images, video and sound.

How Links Work

When viewing a Web page, readers can immediately view another Web page by selecting a link. A link will look different than the surrounding text or images. Most links let readers connect to other pages that relate to the page they are viewing.

URLs

Each page on the Web has a unique address. The address of each page is called the Uniform Resource Locator (URL). The URL for a Web page starts with http and contains the computer name, directory name and name of the Web page.

HOW TO LINK

Link to Other Web Pages

When you want to include a link to a Web page that is not part of your collection, type the complete URL for the page.

http://www.si.edu/start.htm

Link to Your Own Web Pages

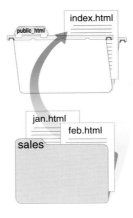

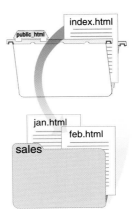

When you want to include a link to a Web page that is located in the same directory, type the name of the page (example: jan.html).

When you want to include a link to a Web page that is located in the top (root) directory, type a slash (/) before the name of the page (example: /index.html).

When you want to include a link to a Web page that is located in a subdirectory, type the name of the subdirectory, followed by a slash (/) and the name of the page (example: sales/feb.html).

Links are one of the most important features on the Web. You can use links to provide your readers with easy access to an unlimited range of information.

Related Web Pages

You can include links to let readers connect to Web pages that relate to your pages. This lets readers quickly access information that other people have already made available on the Web.

Navigate Through Web Pages

You can use links to connect Web pages you have created. Navigational links allow readers to move back and forth through Web pages. Navigational links are the most common type of link on the Web.

Send E-Mail

Sometimes you will want readers to give you feedback. You can include a link on a Web page that lets readers send comments by e-mail.

Related Discussion Groups

A Web page can include a link to a discussion group, or newsgroup, that relates to the topic of your Web page.

Get Files

File Transfer Protocol (FTP) sites allow readers to get files. You can use an FTP link to make software or information easily accessible to your readers.

Definition Links

Definition links help readers who do not know the meaning of a word or phrase in your Web page. A definition link will take readers to a footnote or brief explanation.

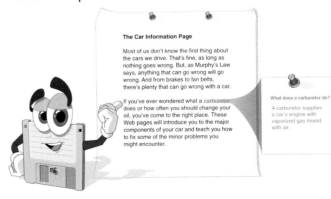

LINK TO ANOTHER WEB PAGE

You can have a word or phrase in your Web page link to another page on the Web. A text link looks different than the text surrounding the link.

CREATE A TEXT LINK

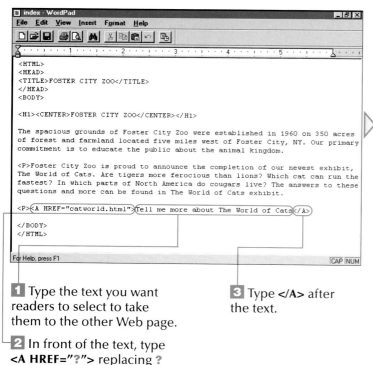

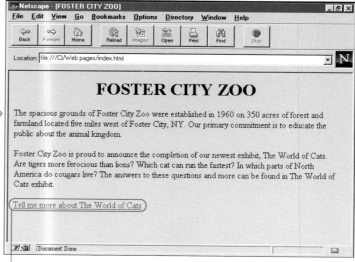

1 Type the text you want readers to select to take them to the other Web page.

2 In front of the text, type **<A HREF="?">** replacing **?** with the location of the Web page you want to link to.

3 Type **</A>** after the text.

■ The Web browser displays the text link in a different color with an underline.

You can have an image in your Web page link to another page on the Web. An image link often displays a border.

CREATE AN IMAGE LINK

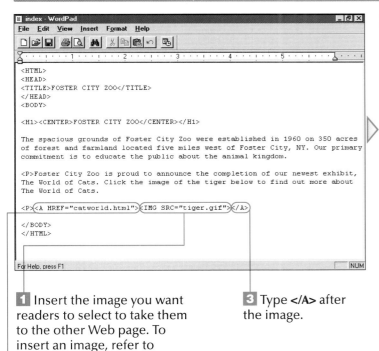

```
<HTML>
<HEAD>
<TITLE>FOSTER CITY ZOO</TITLE>
</HEAD>
<BODY>

<H1><CENTER>FOSTER CITY ZOO</CENTER></H1>

The spacious grounds of Foster City Zoo were established in 1960 on 350 acres
of forest and farmland located five miles west of Foster City, NY. Our primary
commitment is to educate the public about the animal kingdom.

<P>Foster City Zoo is proud to announce the completion of our newest exhibit,
The World of Cats. Click the image of the tiger below to find out more about
The World of Cats.

<P><A HREF="catworld.html"><IMG SRC="tiger.gif"></A>

</BODY>
</HTML>
```

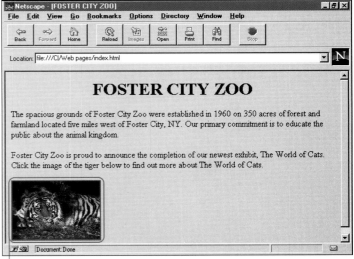

1 Insert the image you want readers to select to take them to the other Web page. To insert an image, refer to page 102.

2 In front of the image, type **<A HREF="?">** replacing **?** with the location of the Web page you want to link to.

3 Type **</A>** after the image.

■ The Web browser displays the image link with a border.

■ To remove the border from the image, set the border thickness to 0. To do so, refer to page 105.

You can provide links to quickly take readers to other sections of a long Web page. This lets readers avoid having to scroll all the way through the page to find an area of interest.

LINK WITHIN A WEB PAGE

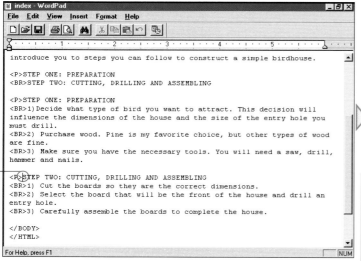

NAME WEB PAGE AREA

1 Position the cursor in front of the area that you want readers to be able to quickly jump to.

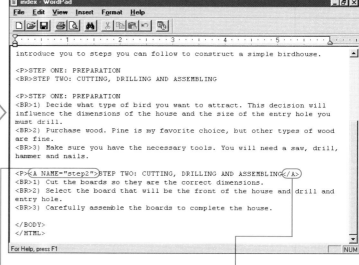

2 Type **<A NAME="?">** replacing **?** with a name that describes that area of the Web page. The name you choose must contain only letters and numbers (A to Z and 0 to 9).

3 Type **</A>** to complete the tag.

Place Link in Web Page

You must add the text or image you want readers to select to take them to another area of the page.

Name Web Page Area

You must name the area of the page that you want readers to be able to quickly jump to.

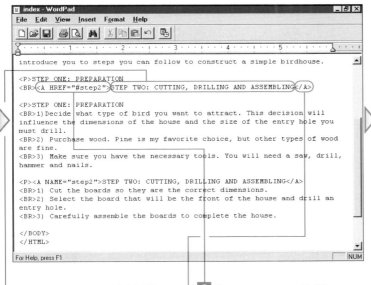

PLACE LINK IN WEB PAGE

1 Position the cursor in front of the text or image you want readers to select to take them to another area of the Web page.

2 Type **<A HREF="#?">** replacing **?** with the name you assigned to the area of the page.

3 Type **</A>** after the text or image.

■ The Web browser displays the link in the Web page.

■ When a reader selects the link, the area of the page you specified appears on the screen.

You can place a link in your Web page to let readers quickly send an e-mail message to you or the person who maintains your Web pages. This is a great way to gather comments about your pages.

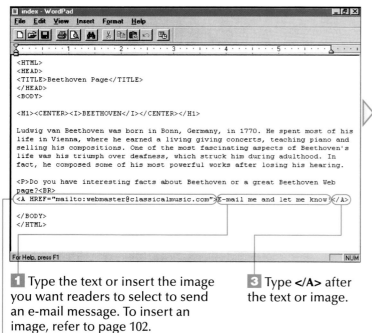

1 Type the text or insert the image you want readers to select to send an e-mail message. To insert an image, refer to page 102.

2 In front of the text or image, type **<A HREF="mailto:?">** replacing **?** with the e-mail address of the person you want to receive the messages.

3 Type **</A>** after the text or image.

■ The Web browser displays the e-mail link in the Web page.

■ When a reader selects the link, their e-mail program will start.

E-MAIL LINK TIPS

E-Mail Programs

When a reader selects an e-mail link in a Web page, their e-mail program will start. The appropriate address is already filled in to ensure that the message will be sent to the right person.

Some Web browsers do not support the e-mail feature. When a reader selects an e-mail link in one of these browsers, an e-mail program will not start.

Use E-Mail Links for Feedback

Make sure each of your Web pages includes an e-mail link to you or the person who maintains your Web pages. This will allow readers to submit questions or comments concerning your Web pages more easily.

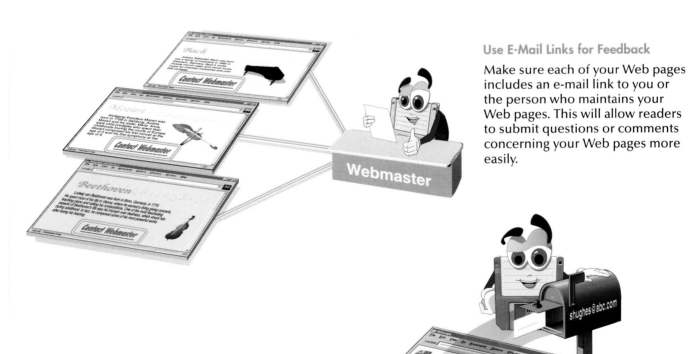

Use E-Mail Links in a Contact Sheet

You can create a Web page that lists the e-mail addresses of people in a company or organization. This makes it very easy for readers to send an e-mail message to the correct person.

You can create a link to a discussion group, or newsgroup, that relates to your Web pages. Newsgroups allow people with common interests to communicate with each other.

There are thousands of newsgroups on every subject imaginable. Each newsgroup has a unique name.

LINK TO A NEWSGROUP

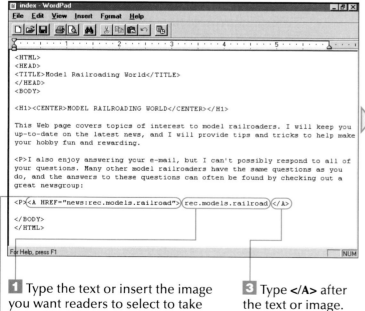

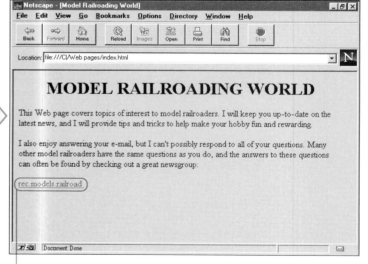

1 Type the text or insert the image you want readers to select to take them to the newsgroup. To insert an image, refer to page 102.

2 In front of the text or image, type **<A HREF="news:?">** replacing **?** with the name of the newsgroup.

3 Type **</A>** after the text or image.

■ The Web browser displays the newsgroup link in the Web page.

■ When a reader selects the link, their newsreader will start and display the articles in the newsgroup.

NEWSGROUP LINK TIPS

Newsreaders

When a reader selects a newsgroup link, their newsreader will start. A newsreader is a program that lets you read and send articles, or messages, to a newsgroup.

Some Web browsers do not support the newsgroup feature. When a reader selects a newsgroup link in one of these browsers, a newsreader will not start.

Available Newsgroups

The articles in newsgroups are stored on computers called news servers. There are thousands of news servers on the Internet and each news server can store different newsgroups.

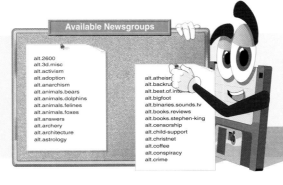

When linking to newsgroups, keep in mind that the newsgroups available to you may not be available to all of your readers.

Available Articles

The articles on a news server take up space. In order for a news server to accept new articles, old articles must be deleted.

When including a newsgroup link in your Web pages, remember that the articles you want readers to view may no longer be available.

FTP sites store huge collections of files that anyone can copy. You can place FTP links on your Web pages to give readers quick access to FTP sites that store files of interest.

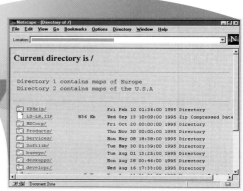

LINK TO AN FTP SITE

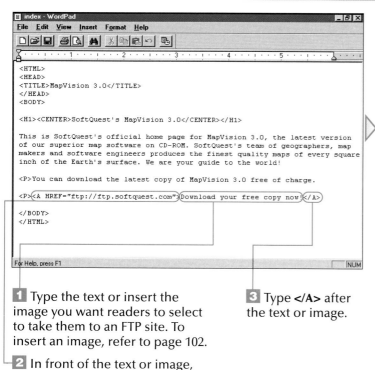

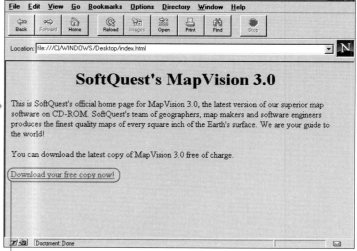

1 Type the text or insert the image you want readers to select to take them to an FTP site. To insert an image, refer to page 102.

2 In front of the text or image, type **<A HREF="?">** replacing **?** with the address of the FTP site.

3 Type **</A>** after the text or image.

■ The Web browser displays the FTP link.

■ When readers select the link, the FTP site you specified will appear.

■ Some Web browsers do not support the FTP feature. When a reader selects an FTP link in one of these browsers, the FTP site will not appear.

You can change the color of visited and unvisited links on your Web pages. Make sure the colors you choose for these links are different and easy to see on your Web pages.

You can get a list of colors at the maranGraphics Web site:

http://www.maran.com/colorchart

CHANGE LINK COLORS

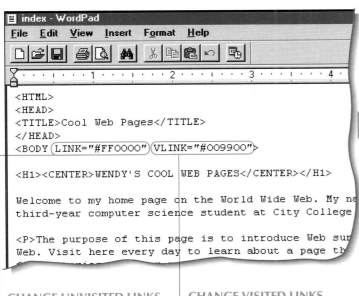

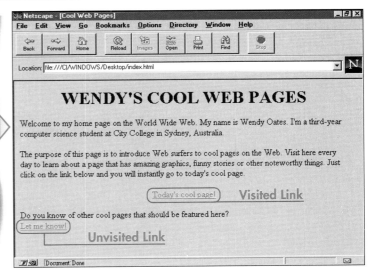

CHANGE UNVISITED LINKS

1 In the <BODY> tag, type **LINK="?"** replacing **?** with the code for the color you want to use (example: LINK="#FFOOOO").

CHANGE VISITED LINKS

1 In the <BODY> tag, type **VLINK="?"** replacing **?** with the code for the color you want to use (example: VLINK="#OO99OO").

■ The Web browser displays the visited and unvisited links in the new colors.

Note: The color of a visited link may not change until after you publish your page on the Web.

LINK CONSIDERATIONS

Links are the tools that hold the Web together. There are some important factors to keep in mind while planning and maintaining the links on your Web pages.

Be Descriptive

When creating a text link, choose a word or phrase that describes the Web page you are linking to. Do not use the phrase "Click Here" for a link.

This phrase forces readers to examine all the surrounding text before they can determine where the link will take them.

Examine Your Links

When you include a link to another Web page, you give readers an opportunity to leave your pages. Make sure that this is really what you want.

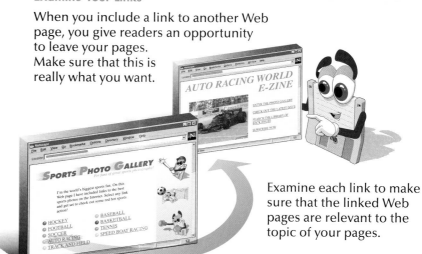

Examine each link to make sure that the linked Web pages are relevant to the topic of your pages.

Check Your Links

If you use links to access Web pages you did not create, you should verify the links on a regular basis. If a reader selects a link that no longer contains relevant information or displays an error message, the reader may assume that all the information on your Web pages is out-of-date.

Notify Readers of Size

Let readers know about any links in your Web pages that will take them to a large Web page. If possible, tell readers the size of the Web page they will be linking to. This allows readers to decide if they want to select the link, since it may take the page a while to transfer.

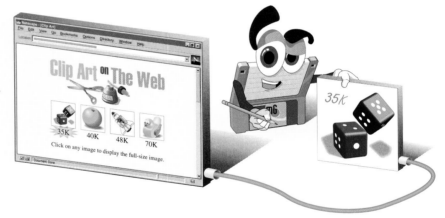

Integrate Links in Web Page

The links in a Web page should not affect how the page is read. The best way to make sure the links do not stand out too much is to print the Web pages. You should be able to read the printed version of your pages without noticing which phrases or words are links.

Separate Links

Do not place two text links beside each other. Text links are usually displayed in a different color and underlined. When two text links are shown side by side, readers may find it difficult to see that there are two separate links, as opposed to one long link.

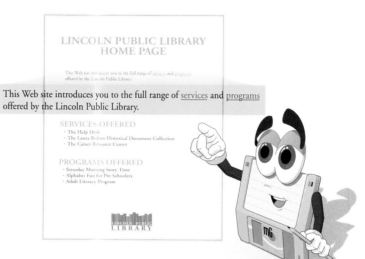

Use Link Menus

If you are going to offer many links in your Web pages, display the links in a menu format, like a table of contents in a book. This neatly displays the links and offers the links in a format that readers are familiar with.

Include Text Descriptions

Make sure that all image links in your Web pages include text descriptions. If you use an image link without a description, it may be hard for readers to determine where the image link will take them.

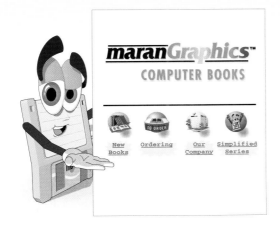

Include Text Links

Some readers turn off the display of images to browse more quickly, while others use browsers that cannot display images. If you use image links, you should also provide text links for these readers.

Use Navigational Links

All your Web pages should include navigational links that allow readers to move through your pages.

Navigational links can include links to a table of contents or to your home page. You can get images to use as navigational links at the following Web sites:

http://www.dgsys.com/~rthonen/ freestuf.html

http://www.cbil.vcu.edu:8080/gifs/ bullet.html

Navigational Link Placement

If you have very long Web pages, place navigational links at both the top and bottom of each page. Readers may become frustrated if they always have to scroll to the top of Web pages they have just read.

TABLES

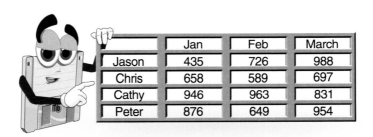

	Jan	Feb	March
Jason	435	726	988
Chris	658	589	697
Cathy	946	963	831
Peter	876	649	954

EMPLOYEE PHONE NUMBERS

Name	Department	Phone Number
Allison, Steve	Accounting	555-1762
Atherly, Peter	Sales	555-2298
Boshart, Mark	Ordering	555-1270
Coleman, Dale	Sales	555-8851
Lang, Kristin	Shipping	555-9993
Lippert, Janet	Accounting	555-0042
Oram, Derek	Maintenance	555-7148
Sanvido, Dean	Service	555-0128
Smith, John	Sales	555-7018
Talbot, Mark	Ordering	555-1510

INTRODUCTION TO TABLES

Tables allow you to control the placement of text and images on your Web pages. Tables may seem complicated, but they are well worth learning how to create.

	Jan	Feb	March
Jason	435	726	988
Chris	658	589	697
Cathy	946	963	831
Peter	876	649	954

You can create a simple table by using the PREFORMAT tag. This tag is also useful for Web browsers that are unable to display tables. For more information on the PREFORMAT tag, refer to page 60.

Table Elements

A table consists of rows, columns and cells.

Last Name	First Name	Street	City
Smith	John	258 Linton Ave.	New York
Lang	Kristin	50 Tree Lane	Boston
Oram	Derek	68 Cracker Ave.	San Francisco
Gray	Russell	401 Idon Dr.	Atlanta
Atherly	Peter	47 Crosby Ave.	Las Vegas
Talbot	Mark	26 Arnold Cres.	Greenwich

Row

A row is a horizontal line of data.

Cell

A cell is the area where a row and column intersect.

Column

A column is a vertical line of data.

Plan Ahead

Tables are often the most confusing part of learning HTML. The key to using tables is to plan the table before adding it to an HTML document. Always sketch your tables on paper before you begin.

USES FOR TABLES

EMPLOYEE PHONE NUMBERS		
Name	**Department**	**Phone Number**
Allison, Steve	Accounting	555-1762
Atherly, Peter	Sales	555-2298
Boshart, Mark	Ordering	555-1270
Coleman, Dale	Sales	555-8851
Lang, Kristin	Shipping	555-9993
Lippert, Janet	Accounting	555-0042
Oram, Derek	Maintenance	555-7148
Sanvido, Dean	Service	555-0128
Smith, John	Sales	555-7018
Talbot, Mark	Ordering	555-1510

Lists of Information

Tables provide a great way to neatly present lists of information. You can use tables to display information such as financial data, telephone listings and price lists.

Newspaper-Style Columns

You can use tables to present information in newspaper-style columns. You can make a table without borders so the structure of the table is invisible. To create a Web page with three newspaper-style columns, place your text in a table that contains one row with three cells.

Borders

You can use a table to place a three-dimensional border around text or an image. A border will make text or an image appear raised above your Web page. To place a border around text or an image, place the text or image in a table that contains one row with one cell.

You can use a table in your Web page to neatly display a list of information.

CREATE A TABLE

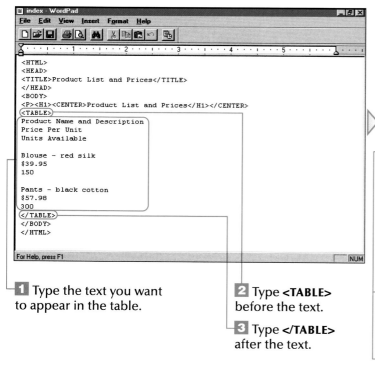

```
<HTML>
<HEAD>
<TITLE>Product List and Prices</TITLE>
</HEAD>
<BODY>
<P><H1><CENTER>Product List and Prices</H1></CENTER>
<TABLE>
Product Name and Description
Price Per Unit
Units Available

Blouse - red silk
$39.95
150

Pants - black cotton
$57.98
300
</TABLE>
</BODY>
</HTML>
```

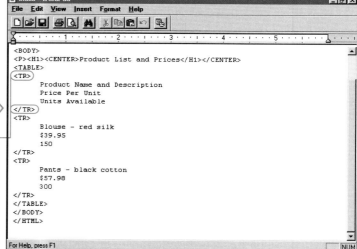

```
<BODY>
<P><H1><CENTER>Product List and Prices</H1></CENTER>
<TABLE>
<TR>
        Product Name and Description
        Price Per Unit
        Units Available
</TR>
<TR>
        Blouse - red silk
        $39.95
        150
</TR>
<TR>
        Pants - black cotton
        $57.98
        300
</TR>
</TABLE>
</BODY>
</HTML>
```

1 Type the text you want to appear in the table.

2 Type **<TABLE>** before the text.

3 Type **</TABLE>** after the text.

4 Type **<TR>** in front of the text you want to appear in one row of the table.

5 Type **</TR>** after the text.

■ You can use tabs to visually separate the elements in the table. This can help you edit the table later. Web browsers will ignore any tabs or extra spaces you place in the table.

When creating a table, you must specify the three main parts of the table.

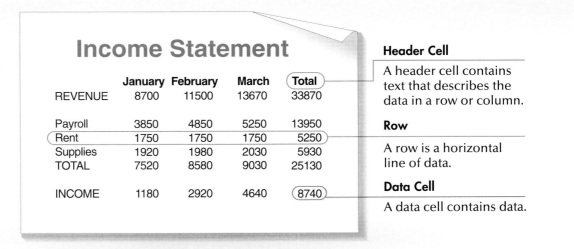

Income Statement

	January	February	March	Total
REVENUE	8700	11500	13670	33870
Payroll	3850	4850	5250	13950
Rent	1750	1750	1750	5250
Supplies	1920	1980	2030	5930
TOTAL	7520	8580	9030	25130
INCOME	1180	2920	4640	8740

Header Cell

A header cell contains text that describes the data in a row or column.

Row

A row is a horizontal line of data.

Data Cell

A data cell contains data.

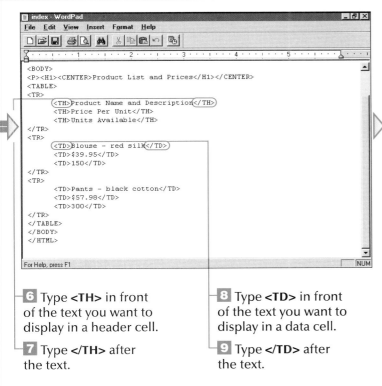

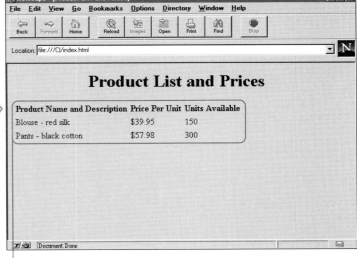

6 Type **<TH>** in front of the text you want to display in a header cell.

7 Type **</TH>** after the text.

8 Type **<TD>** in front of the text you want to display in a data cell.

9 Type **</TD>** after the text.

■ The Web browser displays the table.

CENTER A TABLE

You can horizontally center a table in your Web page.

1 Type **<CENTER>** directly above the <TABLE> tag.

2 Type **</CENTER>** directly below the </TABLE> tag.

You can add a border around your table. A Web browser will also display a line between each cell to make the data easier to read.

	January	February	March	Total
Messenger	800	740	600	2140
Payroll	13850	14850	15250	43950
Rent	1750	1750	1750	5250
Supplies	1920	1980	2030	5930
Computers	7520	8580	9030	25130
Phone	200	250	400	850

	January	February	March	Total
Messenger	800	740	600	2140
Payroll	13850	14850	15250	43950
Rent	1750	1750	1750	5250
Supplies	1920	1980	2030	5930
Computers	7520	8580	9030	25130
Phone	200	250	400	850

ADD A BORDER

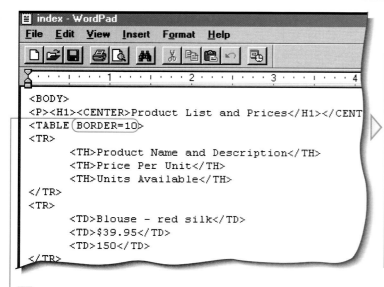

```
<BODY>
<P><H1><CENTER>Product List and Prices</H1></CENT
<TABLE BORDER=10>
<TR>
        <TH>Product Name and Description</TH>
        <TH>Price Per Unit</TH>
        <TH>Units Available</TH>
</TR>
<TR>
        <TD>Blouse - red silk</TD>
        <TD>$39.95</TD>
        <TD>150</TD>
</TR>
```

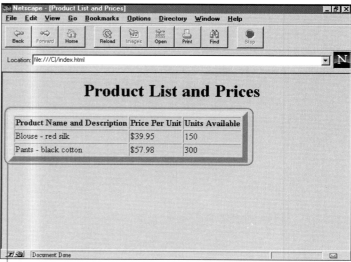

1 In the <TABLE> tag, type **BORDER=?** replacing **?** with the thickness of the border in pixels.

■ The Web browser displays a border around the table. The browser also displays a line between each cell.

ADD A CAPTION

You can add a caption to summarize the information in a table. A Web browser will automatically place the caption above the table.

ADD A CAPTION

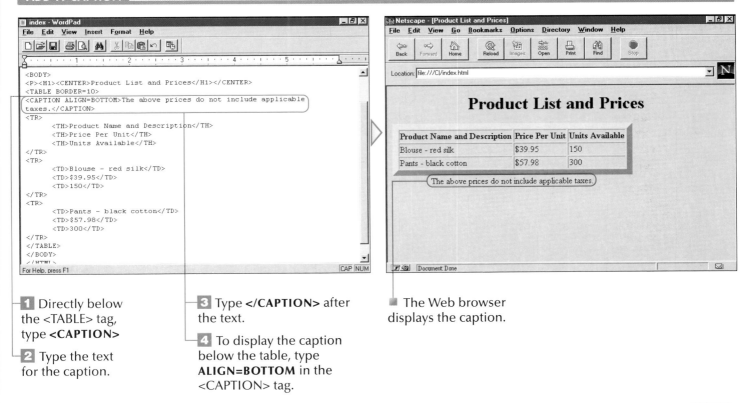

1 Directly below the <TABLE> tag, type **<CAPTION>**

2 Type the text for the caption.

3 Type **</CAPTION>** after the text.

4 To display the caption below the table, type **ALIGN=BOTTOM** in the <CAPTION> tag.

■ The Web browser displays the caption.

SPAN CELLS

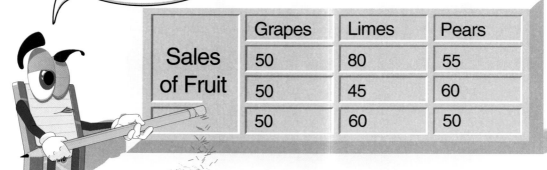

You can combine two or more cells in a column to make one large cell. This is useful if you want to display a title down the side of your table.

Sales of Fruit	Grapes	Limes	Pears
	50	80	55
	50	45	60
	50	60	50

DOWN ROWS

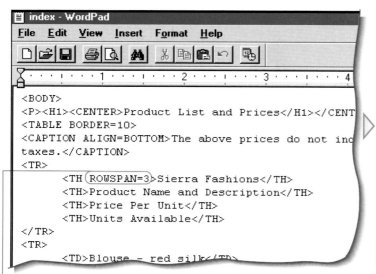

```
<BODY>
<P><H1><CENTER>Product List and Prices</H1></CENT
<TABLE BORDER=10>
<CAPTION ALIGN=BOTTOM>The above prices do not inc
taxes.</CAPTION>
<TR>
        <TH ROWSPAN=3>Sierra Fashions</TH>
        <TH>Product Name and Description</TH>
        <TH>Price Per Unit</TH>
        <TH>Units Available</TH>
</TR>
<TR>
        <TD>Blouse - red silk</TD>
```

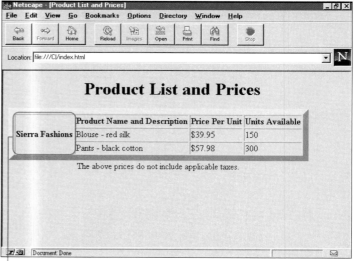

1 In the <TH> or <TD> tag before the cell, type **ROWSPAN=?** replacing **?** with the number of rows you want the cell to span down (example: ROWSPAN=3).

■ The Web browser spans the cell down the number of rows you specified.

ACROSS COLUMNS

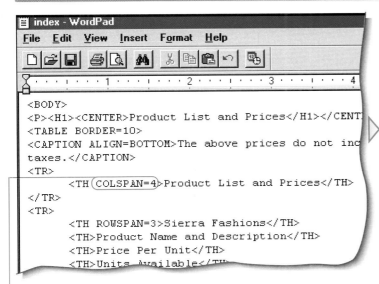

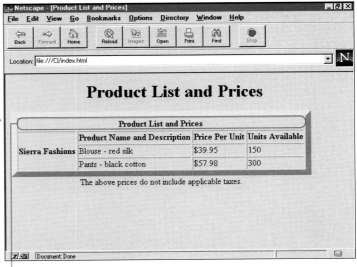

1 In the <TH> or <TD> tag before the cell, type **COLSPAN=?** replacing **?** with the number of columns you want the cell to span across (example: COLSPAN=4).

■ The Web browser spans the cell across the number of columns you specified.

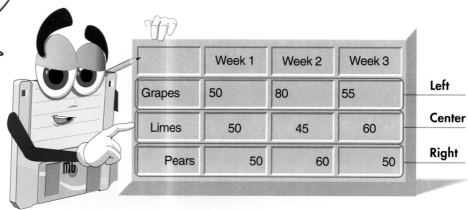

A Web browser automatically centers the data in each cell of a table. You can have the browser left or right align data in each cell. This is useful for aligning a column of numbers.

	Week 1	Week 2	Week 3
Grapes	50	80	55	Left
Limes	50	45	60	Center
Pears	50	60	50	Right

ALIGN DATA HORIZONTALLY

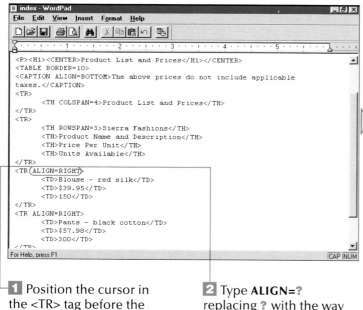

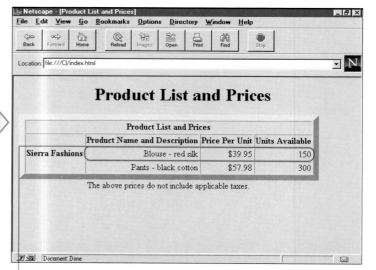

1 Position the cursor in the `<TR>` tag before the row containing the data you want to align horizontally.

2 Type **ALIGN=?** replacing **?** with the way you want to align the data (LEFT, CENTER, RIGHT).

■ The Web browser aligns the data in the row.

■ To align the data in only one cell, repeat steps **1** and **2** in the `<TD>` or `<TH>` tag before the data.

A Web browser automatically places data in the middle of each cell. You can have the browser place the data at the top or bottom of each cell.

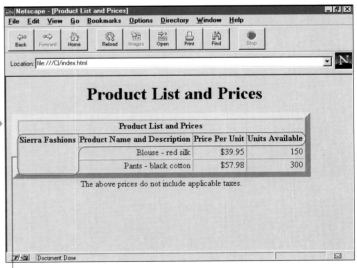

	Week 1	Week 2	Week 3
Grapes	50	80	55	Top
Limes	50	45	60	Middle
Pears	50	60	50	Bottom

ALIGN DATA VERTICALLY

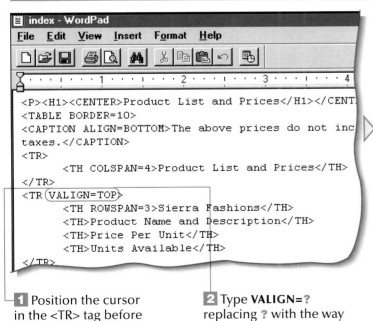

```
<P><H1><CENTER>Product List and Prices</H1></CENT
<TABLE BORDER=10>
<CAPTION ALIGN=BOTTOM>The above prices do not inc
taxes.</CAPTION>
<TR>
        <TH COLSPAN=4>Product List and Prices</TH>
</TR>
<TR VALIGN=TOP>
        <TH ROWSPAN=3>Sierra Fashions</TH>
        <TH>Product Name and Description</TH>
        <TH>Price Per Unit</TH>
        <TH>Units Available</TH>
</TR>
```

Product List and Prices

	Product List and Prices		
Sierra Fashions	Product Name and Description	Price Per Unit	Units Available
	Blouse - red silk	$39.95	150
	Pants - black cotton	$57.98	300

The above prices do not include applicable taxes.

1 Position the cursor in the <TR> tag before the row containing the data you want to align vertically.

2 Type **VALIGN=?** replacing ? with the way you want to align the data (TOP, MIDDLE, BOTTOM).

■ The Web browser aligns the data in the row.

■ To align the data in only one cell, repeat steps **1** and **2** in the <TD> or <TH> tag before the data.

155

PUBLISH WEB PAGES

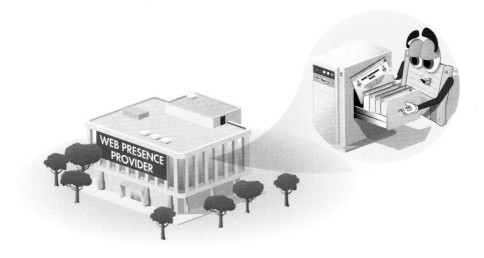

There are many companies that can store your Web pages and make them available all over the world. These companies store thousands of Web pages on computers called Web servers.

Web servers monitor and control access to your Web pages.

Dedicated Web Presence Providers

Dedicated Web presence providers are companies that specialize in storing Web pages. These companies have technical support departments that set up and maintain Web sites. Two of the largest dedicated Web presence providers are:

pair Networks   http://www.pair.com

Digital Landlords   http://www.clever.net

Commercial Online Services

Commercial online services such as America Online, CompuServe and The Microsoft Network publish Web pages created by their customers. Many commercial online services offer easy-to-use programs to help people quickly design and publish their own Web pages.

Internet Service Providers

Internet service providers usually offer a certain amount of space on their Web servers where customers can publish their Web pages. Many Internet service providers offer this space free of charge.

Free Web Servers

If the company that gives you access to the Internet cannot publish your Web pages, there are a few places that will store your Web pages for free. Two of the most popular places to store Web pages for free are:

GeoCities   http://www.geocities.com

Cybertown   http://www.cybertown.com

Your Own Web Server

Purchasing your own Web server is the most expensive way to publish Web pages and requires a full-time connection to the Internet. Setting up and maintaining a Web server is very difficult but gives you the greatest amount of control and flexibility over your Web pages.

A Web presence provider stores Web pages on a computer called a Web server. There are many things you need to consider when selecting a Web presence provider to store your Web pages.

Technical Support

A Web presence provider should have a technical support department to answer your questions. You should be able to contact the department by phone, but the fastest way to contact them is usually by e-mail. A good technical support department will respond to e-mail requests within a day.

Reliability

Make sure the Web server where you are going to store your Web pages is reliable. A Web presence provider should be able to tell you how often the Web server shuts down due to malfunctions. Ask for references from some of the presence provider's customers.

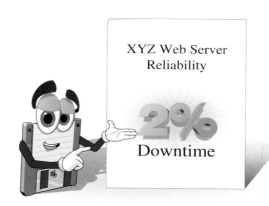

Disk Space

Most Web presence providers limit the amount of space you can use to store your Web pages. Choose a presence provider that lets you store at least 1 MB (megabyte) of information, which is approximately equal to 10 Web pages.

Traffic

Each time someone views one of your Web pages, information transfers to their computer. Some Web presence providers limit the amount of information that can transfer in a day. If more information transfers, you must pay extra. The traffic limit for a small set of Web pages should be at least 50 MB (megabytes) per day, which is approximately equal to 500 Web pages.

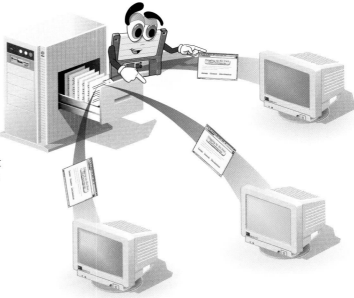

Access Logs

A good Web presence provider will supply you with statistics about your Web pages. You can use these statistics to find out which of your Web pages are popular and where readers are from. Access logs are very useful for determining if you need to make changes to your Web pages.

Domain Name Registration

For a fee, you can choose the address, or domain name, that people type to access your Web pages. A personalized domain name is easier for people to remember and will not change if you switch to another Web presence provider. Most presence providers will register a domain name for you.

E-Mail

A Web presence provider will set up an e-mail account on the same computer system that stores your Web pages. If you already have an e-mail account on another computer system, make sure the presence provider will forward any messages to your existing e-mail account.

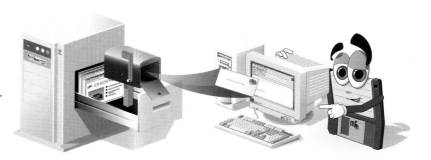

Access

Choose a Web presence provider that lets you transfer your Web pages directly to the Web server. This lets you update your Web pages yourself. Some presence providers allow only their staff to update pages stored on their Web server.

Shell Access

Shell access lets you access your Web pages from any computer connected to the Internet. Shell access is very useful if you plan to update your Web pages from more than one location.

Script Access

Many advanced features found in Web pages, such as questionnaires and online shopping, require programs called scripts. If you plan to use advanced features in your Web pages, make sure the Web presence provider allows you to use scripts.

Database Access

If you want readers to be able to access a large amount of information, such as a product or address list, you can use a database program to store the information. A database program organizes information and allows readers to quickly find information of interest. Look for a Web presence provider that allows you to use a database program.

Many people use search tools to find information on the Web. You can include information in your Web pages to help the search tools better catalog your pages.

SPECIFY KEY WORDS

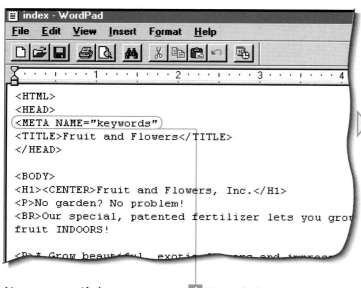

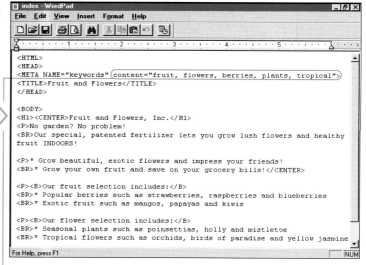

You can specify key words to help search tools categorize your Web page.

1 Directly below the <HEAD> tag, type **<META NAME="keywords"**

2 Press the **Spacebar**. Then type **content="?">** replacing **?** with a list of key words separated by commas.

■ Readers will not see the information in the <META> tag when they view the Web page.

Can I repeat the same key word several times?

Many people repeat the same key word several times in their Web page to improve the chance of their page being selected during a search. Some search tools now penalize Web pages that have a key word repeated more than seven times by ignoring the additional occurrences of the key word.

SPECIFY A DESCRIPTION

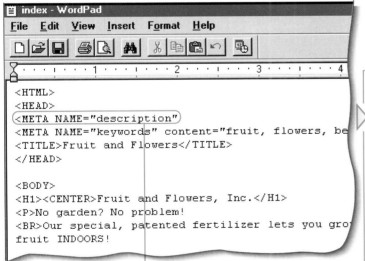

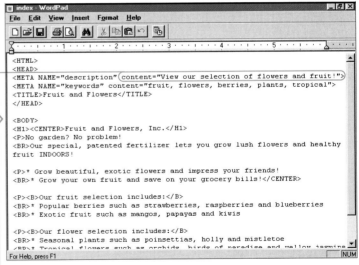

You can include a description you want the search tools to display when they find your Web page.

■1 Directly below the <HEAD> tag, type **<META NAME="description"**

■2 Press the **Spacebar**. Then type **content="?">** replacing **?** with a description of your Web page.

■ Try to use less than 25 words to describe your Web page. Many search tools will display a maximum of 25 words.

PREPARE FILES FOR TRANSFER

Web presence providers have certain rules and restrictions on how you must name and organize your files.

Before transferring files, contact your Web presence provider to get detailed information on their rules and restrictions.

File Names

Some Web presence providers may not accept file names beyond a certain length or file names that include spaces or unusual characters.

Make sure all your files have an extension to indicate the type of file. Web pages have the **.html** or **.htm** extension.

The home page is usually called **index.html** or **welcome.html**

Check File Permissions

Some Web presence providers restrict access to Web pages. If you receive a "Permission Error" when you try to access your Web pages, contact the presence provider to find out how to change the file permissions.

Keep Organized

Find out the name of the directory that will store your files. Most Web servers will store your files in a directory named **public_html**

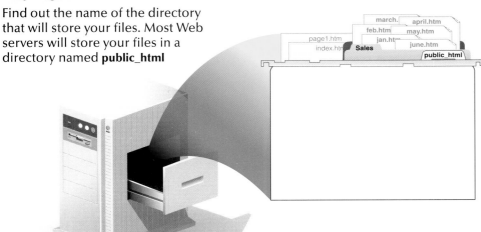

If you have a small number of files, you can place all the files in the public_html directory. If you have a large number of files, you can use subdirectories, or folders, to organize your files.

Check Links

If you place files in different directories, carefully check the links that connect your Web pages to ensure the links still work.

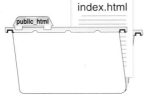

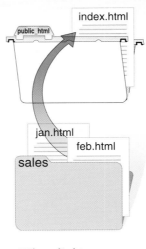

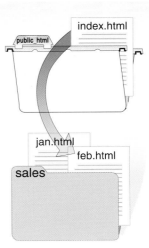

When linking to a file that is located in the same directory, type the name of the file (example: jan.html).

When linking to a file that is located in the top (root) directory, type a slash (/) before the file name (example: /index.html).

When linking to a file that is located in a subdirectory, type the name of the subdirectory, followed by a slash (/) and the file name (example: sales/feb.html).

TRANSFER FILES TO WEB SERVER

> You need to use an FTP program to transfer your Web pages to a Web server. Once the files are on the Web server, your Web pages will be available to everyone on the Web.

You can get these popular FTP programs at the following Web sites:

WS_FTP (Windows)

http://www.ipswitch.com/pd_wsftp.html

Fetch (Macintosh)

http://www.dartmouth.edu/pages/softdev/fetch.html

TRANSFER FILES TO WEB SERVER

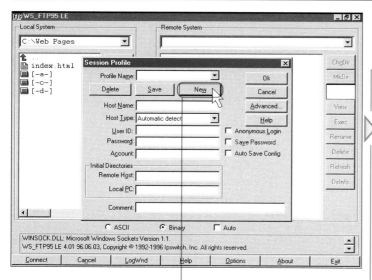

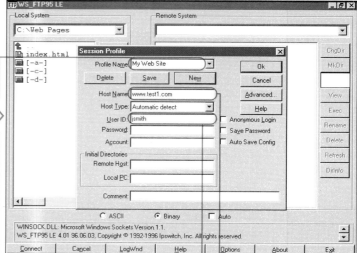

1 Start the program you will use to transfer your files to the Web server (example: WS_FTP).

2 Click **New** to create a new profile. A profile is information you enter to identify the Web pages you want to transfer. If you have more than one set of Web pages, you can give each set a different profile name.

3 In this area, type a name for the profile. You can type any name.

4 In this area, type the name of the Web server you will transfer the files to.

5 In this area, type your user ID.

Before you can transfer files to a Web server, you must know the following information. If you are not sure, ask your Web presence provider.

Host Name

User ID

Password

Directory on Web server where you will store your files

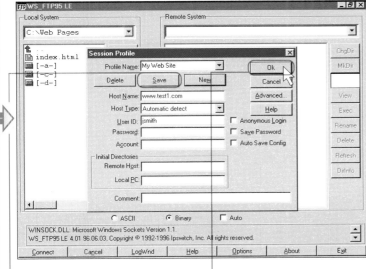

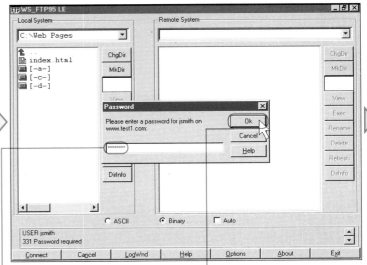

6 Click **Save** to store the information you entered. The next time you use the program, you will not have to perform steps **2** to **6**.

7 Click **Ok**.

■ The **Password** dialog box appears.

8 Type your password. A symbol (x) appears for each character you type.

9 Click **Ok**.

CONTINUED➡

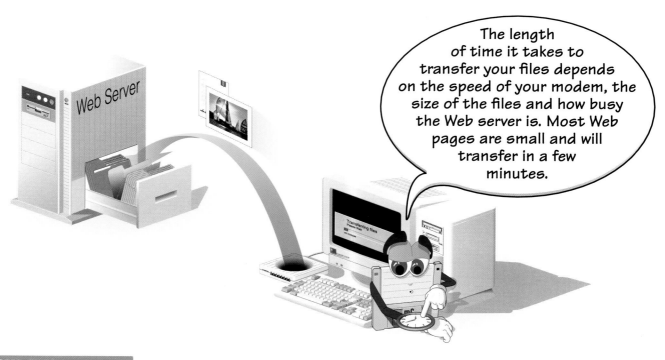

The length of time it takes to transfer your files depends on the speed of your modem, the size of the files and how busy the Web server is. Most Web pages are small and will transfer in a few minutes.

TRANSFER FILES (CONTINUED)

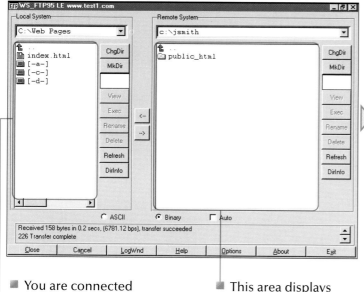

■ You are connected to the Web server.

■ This area displays the contents of your computer.

■ This area displays the contents of the Web server.

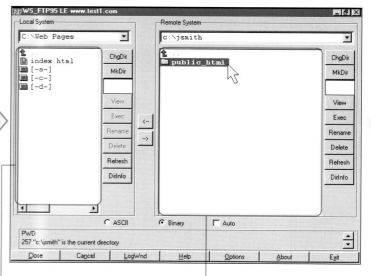

10 In this area, locate the directory that stores the files you want to transfer to the Web server. Then double-click the directory.

11 In this area, locate the directory you want to copy the files to. Then double-click the directory. In most cases, this is the public_html directory.

After I transfer files to the Web server, how do I rename the files?

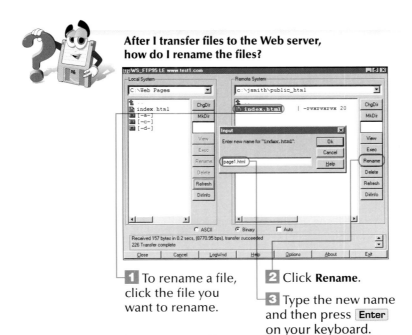

1 To rename a file, click the file you want to rename.

2 Click **Rename**.

3 Type the new name and then press **Enter** on your keyboard.

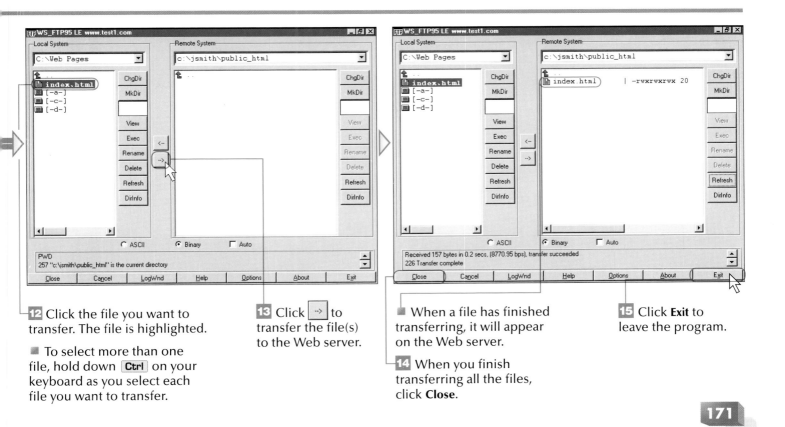

12 Click the file you want to transfer. The file is highlighted.

▪ To select more than one file, hold down **Ctrl** on your keyboard as you select each file you want to transfer.

13 Click →→ to transfer the file(s) to the Web server.

▪ When a file has finished transferring, it will appear on the Web server.

14 When you finish transferring all the files, click **Close**.

15 Click **Exit** to leave the program.

TEST YOUR WEB PAGES

You should carefully test your Web pages to make sure they look and work the way you planned. Many readers will not return to Web pages that contain errors.

Check Spelling

Check the spelling on each of your Web pages before making them available on the Web. Spelling errors will make readers question the amount of effort you put into creating your Web pages. The following Web site will check your pages for spelling errors:

http://www2.imagiware.com/RxHTML

Use Validation Service

Use a validation service on the Web to check all of your Web pages for errors. A validation service will visit your Web pages and notify you of any errors in your use of HTML. One of the most popular validation services is WebTechs, located at:

http://www.webtechs.com

Test Presentation

You should test your Web pages to see how easily you can access and browse through the information. Ensure the Web pages have a consistent design and writing style and also check for formatting and layout errors.

Verify Links

Check all the links in your Web pages to make sure the links take you to the intended destinations. Check links to pages you did not create on a regular basis. This lets you ensure the linked pages still exist and contain information of interest to your readers.

Use a Test Audience

Ask your friends, family members and colleagues with little Web browsing experience to check out your Web pages.

Ask their opinions on the content and design of your Web pages. Compare their comments to a list of your objectives to determine which areas still need work.

Turn Off Images

Some people will view your Web pages with the images turned off or will use Web browsers that cannot display images. Test your Web pages without images to make sure these readers will still find your pages valuable.

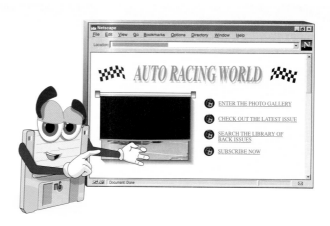

Netscape Navigator

Microsoft Internet Explorer

Try Different Web Browsers

Your Web pages will look different when viewed with different Web browsers. Check your pages on different browsers to make sure the pages look the way you planned. Test your pages with Netscape Navigator and Microsoft Internet Explorer, the two most popular browsers.

Change Web Browser Display

Most Web browsers display bars at the top of the screen to allow you to quickly perform common tasks. In some browsers, these bars can cover almost 15% of the screen. Always test your Web pages with all of the bars displayed to ensure the bars do not hide important information on your pages.

View on Different Computers

Web pages can look and sound very different when displayed on different computers, especially when the pages contain animation. Test your Web pages on different computers to ensure the pages appear the way you intended.

IBM-Compatible   **Macintosh**

640x480

800x600

View at Different Resolutions

The resolution of a monitor determines the amount of information the monitor can display. Readers will view your Web pages at different resolutions. Try viewing your pages at the two most popular resolutions, 640x480 and 800x600.

Modem Speeds

Determine how long it takes for your Web pages to transfer at different modem speeds. If your Web pages contain too much text or too many images, the pages will take a long time to transfer. The most common modem speed is 28,800 bps, but many people still use slower modems to access the Internet.

Once your pages are available on the Web, you need to let the world know about the pages. There is no central location where you can publicize your Web pages, so you must use several methods.

Advertisements

Companies often include Web page addresses in television, radio, newspaper and magazine advertisements. You can also publicize your Web page address on business cards and company letterhead.

Mail Announcement

You can send an announcement about your Web pages to family, friends, colleagues, clients and local newspapers. Find magazines that discuss topics related to your Web pages and send information about your pages to the publications.
When announcing Web pages, emphasize their appeal and give a brief description of the information available.

E-Mail

You can add information about your Web pages to the end of every e-mail message you send. This is a great way to notify people about your Web pages and prevents you from having to type the announcement over and over again. The information you include should be no more than four lines long.

Exchange Links

If another page on the Web discusses ideas related to your Web page, ask if they will include a link to your page if you do the same. This way, people reading the other page can easily visit your page.

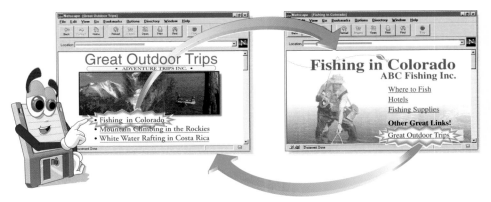

Web Page Banners

Many companies set aside areas on their Web pages where you can advertise your pages. The Internet Link Exchange helps you advertise your Web pages free of charge. The Internet Link Exchange is located at:

http://www.linkexchange.com

Search Tools

You can have your Web pages added to the catalogs of various search tools on the Web. Search tools help people search for a specific topic or browse through categories to find Web pages of interest.

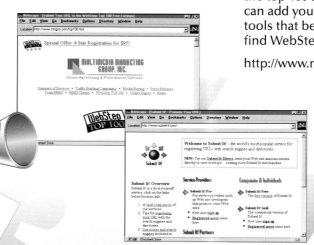

WebStep TOP 100 provides descriptions of the top 100 search tools on the Web. You can add your Web pages to the search tools that best fit your audience. You can find WebStep at:

http://www.mmgco.com/top100.html

Submit It! lets you add your Web pages to many search tools at one time. Submit It! is located at:

http://www.submit-it.com

Robots

Many search tools use programs called robots to scan the Web for new or updated pages. If you do not want robots to search all or some of your Web pages, you can instruct robots to skip the pages. You can learn more about robots at the following Web site:

http://info.webcrawler.com/mak/projects/robots/robots.html

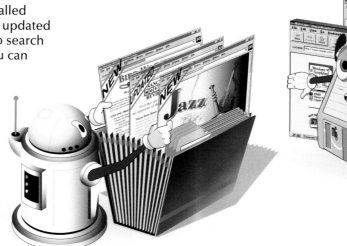

Newsgroups

You can send an announcement of your Web pages to carefully selected discussion groups, called newsgroups. Each newsgroup on the Internet discusses a particular topic.

Read the articles in a newsgroup for a week before sending an announcement. This lets you make sure the topics discussed relate to your Web pages. Sending an announcement to inappropriate newsgroups is called spamming and is not approved of on the Internet.

The following newsgroup lets you announce new or updated Web pages:

comp.infosystems.www.announce

Mailing Lists

You can send an announcement to carefully selected mailing lists. A mailing list is a discussion group that uses e-mail to communicate.

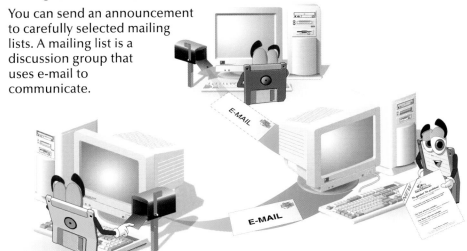

Read the messages in a mailing list for a week before sending an announcement. This lets you make sure the readers of the mailing list would be interested in your Web pages.

You can find a catalog of mailing lists with descriptions at the following Web site:

http://www.neosoft.com/internet/paml

Keep Information Up-to-Date

Make sure you update the information displayed on your Web pages whenever necessary. You can add new ideas, topics or information at any time. Frequently changing the content of your Web pages gives readers a reason to return to your pages.

Use Feedback

Always provide a way for readers to express their thoughts and ask questions about your Web pages. A Web page can include your e-mail address or a form that readers can fill in. Make sure you read and incorporate feedback on a regular basis. Comments from readers provide the best way for you to determine if your pages need updating.

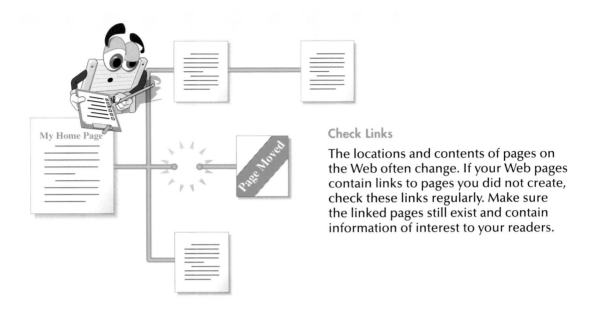

Check Links

The locations and contents of pages on the Web often change. If your Web pages contain links to pages you did not create, check these links regularly. Make sure the linked pages still exist and contain information of interest to your readers.

Examine Access Logs

A Web presence provider can supply you with statistics indicating which of your Web pages are popular and where readers are from. If you have an unpopular Web page, try to determine why. Examine the content and layout of the page for errors and make sure links to the page work.

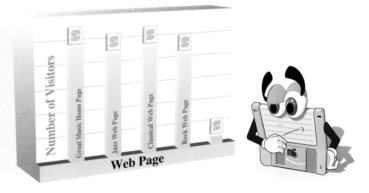

Check HTML Tags

Keep informed about the latest developments in HTML. If your Web pages contain HTML tags that only work with one type of Web browser, make sure the browser still uses those tags. Update your Web pages regularly using the latest HTML tags.

ADVANCED WEB PAGES

SOUND

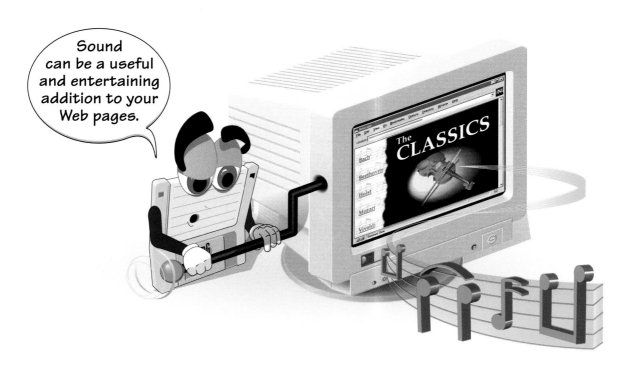

REASONS FOR INCLUDING SOUND

Entertainment

Entertainment is the most popular reason for including sound in Web pages. You can include sound clips from television shows and movies, famous speeches, sound effects, theme songs and much more. Many people visit Web pages just to hear sound, so including sound in your Web pages can attract more visitors.

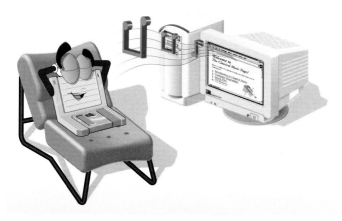

Sales

Sound files are very useful if you are selling audio products such as compact discs or audio tapes. People may be more likely to buy a product if they can first listen to a sample of the product.

WHERE TO GET SOUNDS

The Internet

There are many places on the Internet that offer sounds you can use in your Web pages. You can find sound files at the following Web sites:

http://sunsite.unc.edu:80/pub/multimedia/sun-sounds/movies

http://www.dailywav.com

http://www.hollywood.com/movies/sound.html

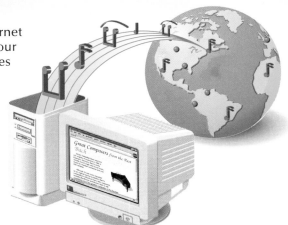

Commercial Sound Clips

Many computer stores sell CD-ROM discs that contain collections of sounds. Each CD-ROM disc provides many sounds that you can use in your Web pages. These sounds usually have no copyright restrictions, so you can use the sounds in your Web pages without needing to get permission.

Record Sounds

If your computer has a sound card, you can record sounds by connecting a CD or cassette player to the computer. Many sound cards come with a microphone so you can also record your own voice. When recording a sound you did not create, make sure you have permission to use the sound in your Web page.

SOUND

TYPES OF SOUND

You will find many types of sound on the Web. You can determine the type of sound by looking at the characters after the period in a file name. The most accepted type of sound is WAVE.

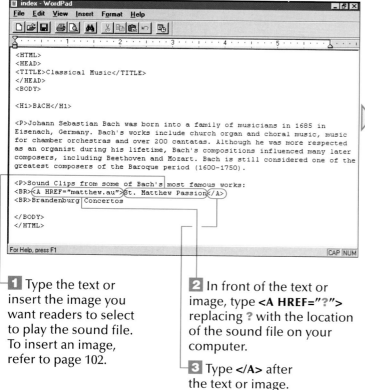

There are programs that can change a sound file to a different type of sound. You can get sound conversion programs at the following Web sites:

GoldWave (Windows)
http://web.cs.mun.ca/~chris3/goldwave

SoundApp (Macintosh)
http://www.wctc.net/new/snd.html

ADD SOUND FILE TO WEB PAGE

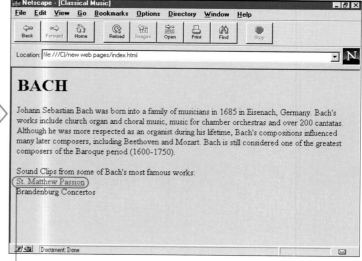

1 Type the text or insert the image you want readers to select to play the sound file. To insert an image, refer to page 102.

2 In front of the text or image, type **<A HREF="?">** replacing **?** with the location of the sound file on your computer.

3 Type **</A>** after the text or image.

■ The Web browser displays the sound link in the Web page.

■ When a reader selects the link, the sound file will transfer to their computer and the sound will play.

Use Small Sound Files

Using small sound files reduces the time it takes for the files to transfer. If a file will take too long to transfer, a reader may decide not to play the sound. You can reduce the size of sound files by keeping the sound clips short.

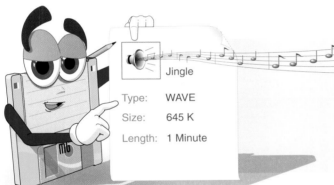

Jingle

Type:	WAVE
Size:	645 K
Length:	1 Minute

Give Descriptions

When providing a link to a sound file, use a phrase or image to indicate that the link will play a sound. You should also include the sound file type and size, as well as the length of time the sound will play. This information allows readers to decide if they want to play the sound.

Sound Alternatives

Some readers may be hearing impaired or have computers that cannot play sound. When providing important information in a sound file, include the information somewhere else on the Web page. For example, if you include a sound file of a speech, also include a text version of the speech.

Adding video to your Web pages is an effective way to present information. You can use video for education, entertainment and advertising.

Types of Video

You will find many types of video on the Web. You can determine the type of video by looking at the characters after the period in a file name. The most accepted type of video file is AVI.

AVI	plane.avi
MPEG	dog.mpg car.mpe
QUICK TIME	bird.qt ball.mov

Where to Get Video

Many computer stores sell CD-ROM discs that contain collections of video. There are also places on the Internet that offer video that you can use in your Web pages. You can find video files at the following Web sites:

http://www.uslink.net/~edgerton/index.html

http://www.univ-rennes1.fr/ASTRO/anim-ewf.html

You can create your own personalized video with a special video card and video camera.

VIDEO CONSIDERATIONS

Use Small Video Files

Video files tend to be the largest files found on the Web. Large files can take a long time to transfer, which can frustrate readers. Try to keep videos short to reduce the time it takes the files to transfer.

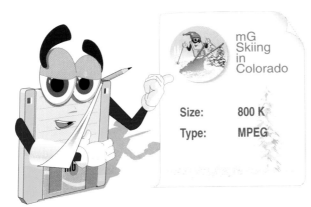

Give Descriptions

When providing a link to a video file, include a short description of the video as well as the file size and type. Readers can use this information to decide if they want to transfer the video.

Be Selective

Carefully examine the videos you want to include in your Web pages and decide whether or not each video is really needed. Make sure the videos are relevant to the information in your pages.

FORMS

> Including forms on your Web pages allows readers to send you information.

HOW FORMS WORK

Getting Information

Readers can quickly fill out a form by selecting check boxes, choosing menu options or typing information such as a name or address. When readers finish selecting options and entering information, they select a "Submit" button to transfer the information to the Web server.

Processing Information

When a Web server receives information from a form, the server runs a program called a Common Gateway Interface (CGI) script. CGI scripts convert the information into details that the owner of the Web site can understand. Before including forms in your Web pages, ask your Web presence provider if the Web server can run CGI scripts.

REASONS FOR USING FORMS

Questionnaires

Forms are an excellent way to gather information from readers. Many companies use forms to find out about the people who visit their Web pages.

Shopping

Many companies use large, complex forms to allow their readers to purchase products and services over the Web. These companies use expensive security programs to protect the information people enter into forms.

Technical Support

Companies often include forms on their Web pages to allow readers to submit questions about products and services. When a reader submits a question, the CGI script will forward the question to the correct person.

Feedback

Most companies use forms to allow readers to express their opinions. Check boxes and menus help readers quickly fill out forms.

Frames split a Web browser screen into different sections. Each section can display a separate Web page.

When designing your Web site, keep in mind that some people use Web browsers that cannot display frames.

Using Frames

Try not to use too many frames in your Web pages since this may display too much information at once and confuse readers. Using frames also shrinks the display size of each Web page.

Resize Frames

Readers can resize some frames by using the mouse to drag the edge of a frame to a new position. Resizing frames lets readers control the amount of information displayed in each Web page.

Scroll Bars

Some frames may be too small to display all the contents of a Web page. Frames often have scroll bars to allow readers to move through long Web pages.

REASONS FOR USING FRAMES

Headers

Frames let you display a banner or logo at the top of the screen. The banner will always be visible while readers browse through your Web pages.

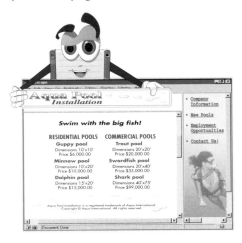

Navigation

You can place a table of contents, navigational tools or search tools in a frame to keep them on the screen at all times. This helps readers easily move through your Web pages and find information of interest.

Forms

You can have one frame in your Web page display a form and another frame display the results. When readers fill out the form, they can view their input and the results at the same time.

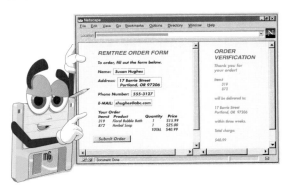

Important Information

You can use frames to display important information all the time. This is ideal for information such as warning messages and copyright notices.

IMAGEMAPS

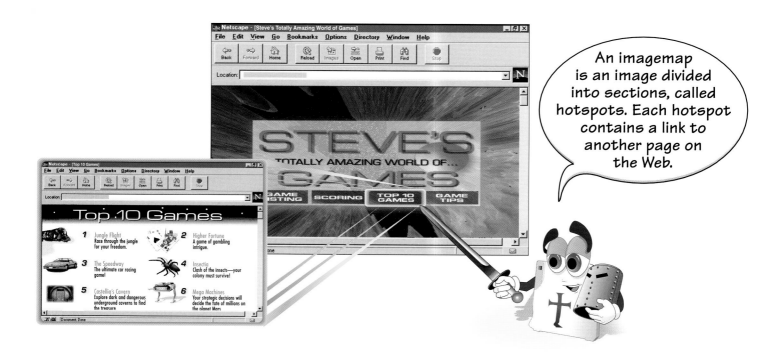

An imagemap is an image divided into sections, called hotspots. Each hotspot contains a link to another page on the Web.

TYPES OF IMAGEMAPS

Menu Bars

A menu bar is a popular type of imagemap containing several areas that link readers to other Web pages. The areas can be text or small pictures.

Maps

You can turn a map into an imagemap. Each area on the map can link to a Web page containing information about the area. Floor plans, campus maps and world maps are commonly used as imagemaps.

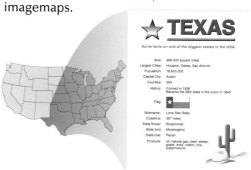

IMAGEMAP CONSIDERATIONS

Use Well-Defined Images

The best images to use for imagemaps have several distinct areas that readers can select. Photographs often do not make good imagemaps since they do not have well-defined areas.

Describe Imagemaps

Make sure readers know where each link in an imagemap will take them. When creating an imagemap, include text describing each link. For example, do not assume readers know that an image of a house links to your home page.

Provide Text Links

Some readers turn off the display of images to browse more quickly, while others use Web browsers that cannot display images. Include text links below the imagemap to ensure the imagemap links are also available for these readers.

VRML

Virtual Reality Modeling Language (VRML) allows you to create three-dimensional objects and environments, called VRML worlds.

VRML Viewers

A VRML viewer lets readers use a mouse or keyboard to move through three-dimensional areas or walk around objects in a VRML world. To display a VRML world, a Web browser must support VRML. Most new browsers support VRML.

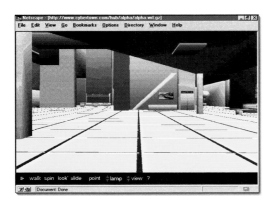

VRML Editors

Creating VRML worlds requires a lot of time. A VRML editor is a program that can help you create VRML worlds. One of the most popular VRML editors is Caligari Pioneer, which is available at the following Web site:

http://www.caligari.com

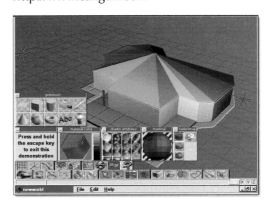

REASONS FOR USING VRML

Entertainment

You can use VRML to create three-dimensional towns, movies and games. When playing a VRML game, you can compete against other people on the Web.

You can find entertaining VRML worlds at the following Web sites:

http://www.cybertown.com/3dvd.html

http://www.virtualvegas.com/vrml/vrml1.html

Product Demonstrations

Companies often use VRML to show their products. You can walk around products and view them from any angle. This gives you control that you do not have when viewing television or magazine advertisements.

Two companies that allow you to view their products using VRML are:

http://www.netvision.net.il/~teldor/vrml.html

http://www.asia-online.com.sg/perfection/es300/features.html

Training

In the future, there will be VRML worlds that allow people to use the Internet to train at home instead of going to a classroom.

Companies will also create VRML worlds to provide instruction on tasks such as servicing electronic products or repairing cars.

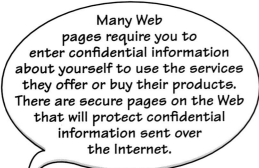

Many Web pages require you to enter confidential information about yourself to use the services they offer or buy their products. There are secure pages on the Web that will protect confidential information sent over the Internet.

When you send information over the Internet, the information may pass through many computers before reaching its destination.

If you are not connected to a secure Web page, people may be able to view the information you send.

Secure Web Pages

Secure Web pages work with Web browsers that support security features to create an almost unbreakable security system. When you connect to a secure Web page, other people on the Internet cannot view the information you transfer.

Visit Secure Web Pages

When a reader visits a secure Web page, the Web browser will usually display a solid key or a lock at the bottom corner of the screen. This indicates that the Web page is secure.

Microsoft Internet Explorer

Netscape Navigator

REASONS FOR USING SECURITY

Shopping

You can order many products on the Web. Many companies require you to enter credit card information to buy their products. Companies use secure Web pages so you can safely send credit card information over the Web. Most companies also allow you to send your credit card information by phone or fax.

Companies

Some people work at home and use the Internet to connect to computers at the office. Secure Web pages allow employees to access confidential information that companies would not make available over connections that are not secure.

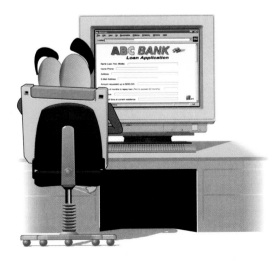

Banking

Many banks allow you to access your banking information over the Web. You can pay bills, transfer money between accounts and even apply for a loan. Banking information is one of the most confidential types of information. Banks use secure Web pages to keep this information secret.

> Java is a programming language that allows you to create animated and interactive Web pages.

A Java program used in a Web page is called a Java applet. You can write a Java applet yourself or use one of the existing applets available on the Web.

How Java Works

Java applets are stored on a Web server. When a reader displays a Web page containing a Java applet, the applet transfers from the Web server to the reader's computer and then runs. Some Java applets take a long time to transfer.

Web Browsers

Before viewing a Java applet on a Web page, a reader must have a Web browser that can run Java applets. Most new Web browsers can run Java applets.

Java applets can run on many different types of computer systems, such as Macintosh, Windows and Unix.

REASONS FOR USING JAVA

Web Page Enhancements

Most people use Java applets to enhance their Web pages. Many applets are used to display moving text or simple animation. You can view a collection of Java applets at the following Web site:

http://www.gamelan.com

Interactive Web Pages

You can use Java applets in your Web pages to allow readers to interact with each other on the Web. Some Java applets allow readers to play games or chat with other people.

Programs

You can use Java to write complex programs such as word processing, spreadsheet and drawing programs. These types of Java applets are very large. Most people do not include this type of Java applet in their Web pages because the applets take too long to transfer.

JAVASCRIPT

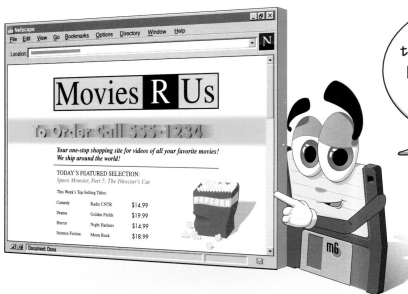

JavaScript is a programming language that is mainly used for Web page enhancements, such as displaying scrolling messages and fading-in Web pages.

Although the names are similar, JavaScript and Java have very little in common. JavaScript is easier to learn than Java.

How JavaScript Works

JavaScript instructions are placed in the HTML document. You can write JavaScript instructions yourself or use existing JavaScript instructions available on the Web. You can view examples of JavaScript at the following Web site:

http://www.gamelan.com

Web Browsers

Before viewing JavaScript on a Web page, a reader must have a Web browser that can run JavaScript instructions. Most new Web browsers can run JavaScript.

ActiveX is a newer technology developed by Microsoft to help you improve your Web pages.

Reasons for Using ActiveX

ActiveX is commonly used in Web pages to add pop-up menus that instantly display a list of options.

You can also use ActiveX to include animated images and information from popular programs, such as Microsoft Word or Microsoft Excel, in your Web pages.

Web Browsers

Before viewing a Web page that includes ActiveX features, a reader must have a Web browser that supports ActiveX. Microsoft Internet Explorer has built-in support for ActiveX.

Some Web browsers, including Netscape Navigator, currently do not have built-in support. Readers who want to use ActiveX with Netscape Navigator can get a special program at the following Web site:

http://www.ncompasslabs.com

STYLE SHEETS

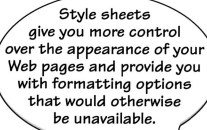

> Style sheets give you more control over the appearance of your Web pages and provide you with formatting options that would otherwise be unavailable.

You can find out more about style sheets at the following Web site:

http://www.microsoft.com/workshop/author/howto/css-f.htm

How Style Sheets Work

Style sheets allow you to specify exactly how you want text and images to appear. You can create sophisticated Web pages that look like pages from a magazine. You can use style sheets to define the design you want to use in a section of a Web page, an entire Web page or all of your Web pages.

Web Browsers

Before you can view Web pages that use style sheets, you need a Web browser that supports style sheets. Most new Web browsers can display Web pages that use style sheets.

REASONS FOR USING STYLE SHEETS

Appearance

Style sheets allow you to create impressive Web pages without greatly increasing the file size of the pages. You can use style sheets to control the exact layout and formatting of your Web pages. You can specify the font size, line spacing, background colors, page margins and location of information on the screen.

Easy to Update

Style sheets allow you to give all your Web pages a consistent style. You can use a style sheet to define the formatting and layout you want to use for several Web pages. You can change the style sheet to easily change the appearance of all your pages at once.

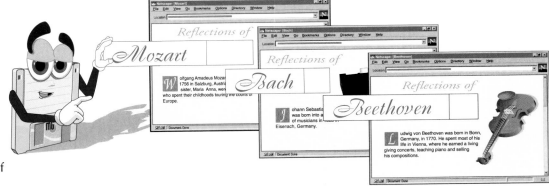

Microsoft Internet Explorer

Netscape Navigator

Consistency

Web pages can look very different when displayed on different Web browsers. Web pages that use style sheets will appear the same no matter which browser displays the pages.

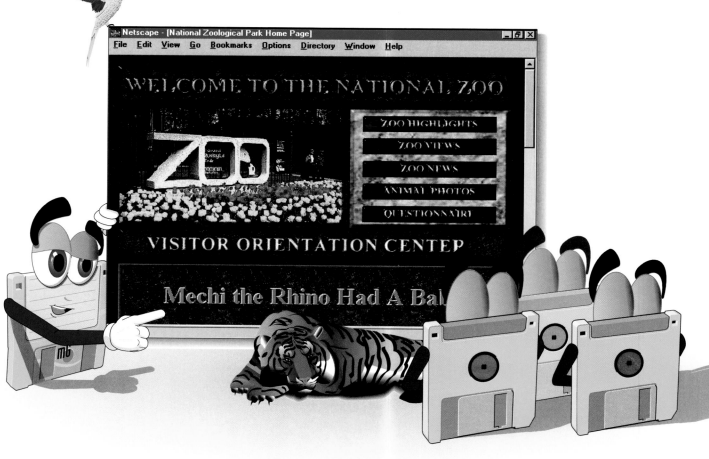

GREAT WEB SITES

You can browse through these Web sites to get ideas for your own Web pages.

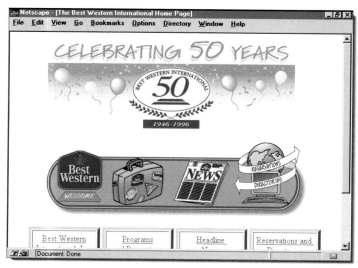

Best Western
URL http://www.bestwestern.com/best.html

Campbell Soup Company
URL http://www.campbellsoups.com

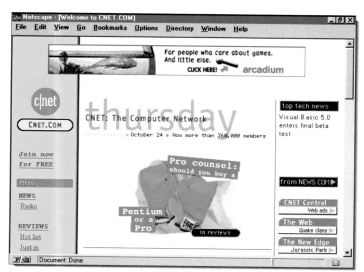

CNET: The Computer Network
URL http://www.cnet.com

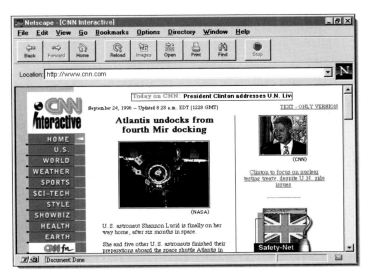

CNN Interactive
URL http://www.cnn.com

Consumer Direct Electronics
URL http://www.wholesalece.com

CyberDance
URL http://www.thepoint.net/~raw/dance.htm

Discovery Channel Online
URL http://www.discovery.com

ESPNET SportsZone
URL http://espnet.sportszone.com

Flower Stop
URL http://www.flowerstop.com

golf.com
URL http://www.golf.com

Hotels and Travel on the Net
URL http://www.hotelstravel.com

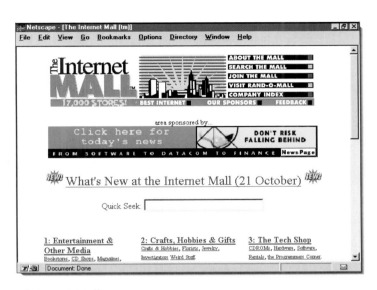

Internet Mall
URL http://www.internet-mall.com

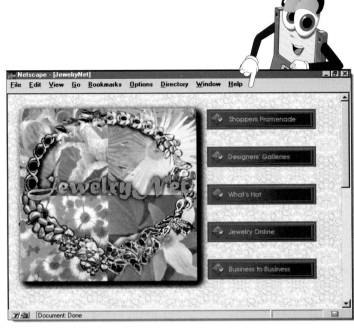

JewelryNet
URL http://www.jewelrynet.com

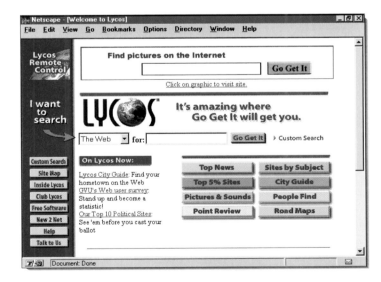

Lycos
URL http://www.lycos.com

MovieWEB
URL http://movieweb.com/movie/movie.html

GREAT WEB SITES

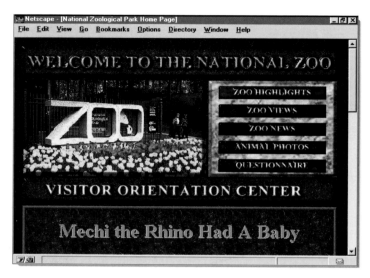

National Zoo
URL http://www.si.edu/natzoo

Pathfinder
URL http://www.pathfinder.com

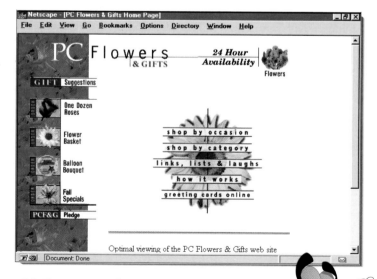

PC Flowers & Gifts
URL http://www.pcflowers.com

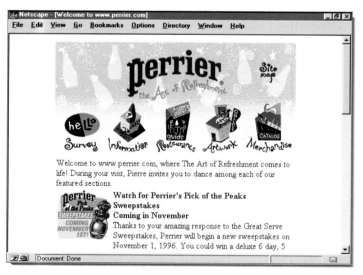

Perrier
URL http://www.perrier.com

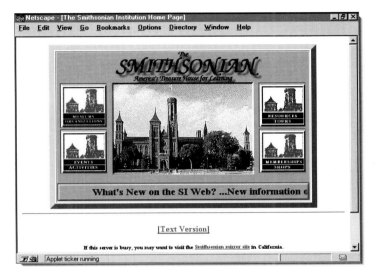

Smithsonian Institution
URL http://www.si.edu

Spiegel
URL http://www.spiegel.com

USA Today
URL http://www.usatoday.com

Veggies Unite!
URL http://vegweb.com

INDEX

INDEX

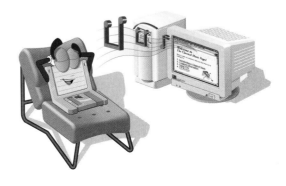

INDEX

COMMON HTML TAGS

TAG FUNCTION, PAGE NUMBER	OPENING TAG & ATTRIBUTES	CLOSING TAG
CHARACTER FORMATTING		
Block quote, 74	<BLOCKQUOTE>	</BLOCKQUOTE>
Bold text, 70	<B>	</B>
Font (section of text)	<FONT>	</FONT>
Color, 78	COLOR="color code"	
Size, 76	SIZE="1 to 7"	
Italicize text, 70	<I>	</I>
Preformatted text, 60	<PRE>	</PRE>
Strike out text, 71	<STRIKE>	</STRIKE>
Subscript text, 73	<SUB>	</SUB>
Superscript text, 73	<SUP>	</SUP>
Typewriter text, 72	<TT>	</TT>

IMAGES

Image, add, 102	<IMG SRC="image location">	
Align, 112	ALIGN=LEFT, RIGHT	
Align text beside image, 114	ALIGN=TOP, MIDDLE, BOTTOM	
Alternative text, add, 104	ALT="text"	
Border, 105	BORDER=number	
Height, 110, 111	HEIGHT=number	
Space above and below image, 115	VSPACE=number	
Space beside image, 115	HSPACE=number	
Width, 110, 111	WIDTH=number	
Text, stop wrap, 113	<BR CLEAR=LEFT, RIGHT, ALL>	

TAG FUNCTION, PAGE NUMBER	OPENING TAG & ATTRIBUTES	CLOSING TAG

DOCUMENT STRUCTURE

Body of document, 55	<BODY>	</BODY>
Document head, 54	<HEAD>	</HEAD>
HTML document, 54	<HTML>	</HTML>
Title of document, 55	<TITLE>	</TITLE>

DOCUMENT FORMATTING

Body of document, 55	<BODY>	</BODY>
Background color, 80	BGCOLOR="color code"	
Background image, 106	BACKGROUND="image location"	
Font color (entire document), 79	TEXT="color code"	
Center item, 64, 103, 149	<CENTER>	</CENTER>
Font size (entire document), 77	<BASEFONT SIZE="1 to 7">	
Heading, add, 61	<H1 to 6>	</H1 to 6>
Align, 65	ALIGN=LEFT, CENTER, RIGHT	
Horizontal rule, add, 96	<HR>	
Align, 98	ALIGN=LEFT, CENTER, RIGHT	
No shade, 97	NOSHADE	
Thickness, 97	SIZE=number	
Width, 98	WIDTH="number%"	
Line, start new, 59	 	
Paragraph, start new, 58	<P>	
Align, 65	ALIGN=LEFT, CENTER, RIGHT	

COMMON HTML TAGS

TAG FUNCTION, PAGE NUMBER	OPENING TAG & ATTRIBUTES	CLOSING TAG

LINKS

TAG FUNCTION, PAGE NUMBER	OPENING TAG & ATTRIBUTES	CLOSING TAG

Body of document, 55
   Unvisited link color, 139
   Visited link color, 139
	\<BODY>
	   LINK="color code"
	   VLINK="color code"
		\</BODY>

Label area in Web page, 132	\<A NAME="label">	\</A>
Link to another item, 118, 130, 131, 138, 186	\<A HREF="item location/URL">	\</A>
Link to e-mail, 134	\<A HREF="mailto:e-mail address">	\</A>
Link to labeled area, 133	\<A HREF="#label">	\</A>
Link to newsgroup, 136	\<A HREF="news:newsgroup name">	\</A>

LISTS

TAG FUNCTION, PAGE NUMBER	OPENING TAG & ATTRIBUTES	CLOSING TAG
Definition list, 85	\<DL>	\</DL>
Definition list definition, 85	\<DD>	
Definition list term, 85	\<DT>	
List item, 82, 84	\<LI>	

Ordered list, 82
   Number style, 83
   Starting number, 83
	\<OL>
	   TYPE=style
	   START=number
		\</OL>

Unordered list, 84	\<UL>	\</UL>

TAG FUNCTION, PAGE NUMBER	OPENING TAG & ATTRIBUTES	CLOSING TAG

TABLES

TAG FUNCTION, PAGE NUMBER	OPENING TAG & ATTRIBUTES	CLOSING TAG
Caption, 151 　Align, 151	<CAPTION> 　ALIGN=TOP, BOTTOM	</CAPTION>
Data cell in table, 149 　Span cells across column, 153 　Span cells down row, 152	<TD> 　COLSPAN=number 　ROWSPAN=number	</TD>
Header cell in table, 149 　Span cells across column, 153 　Span cells down row, 152	<TH> 　COLSPAN=number 　ROWSPAN=number	</TH>
Table, add, 148 　Border, 150	<TABLE> 　BORDER=number	</TABLE>
Table row, 148 　Align text in row, horizontally, 154 　Align text in row, vertically, 155	<TR> 　ALIGN=LEFT, CENTER, RIGHT 　VALIGN=TOP, MIDDLE, BOTTOM	</TR>

OTHER

TAG FUNCTION, PAGE NUMBER	OPENING TAG & ATTRIBUTES
Comment, 75	<!-- text -->
Description for search tools, 165	<META NAME="description" content="text">
Key words for search tools, 164	<META NAME="keywords" content="text">